GRANTA

HOME

23

Editor: Bill Buford
Assistant Editor: Richard Rayner
Managing Editor: Angus MacKinnon
Publisher: George Dillehay
Associate Publisher: Piers Spence
Financial Manager: Monica McStay
Assistant to the Editor: Jean Marray
Subscriptions: Gillian Kemp, Tania Rice
Advertising and Marketing: Alison Ormerod
Design: Chris Hyde
Editorial Assistant: Alicja Kobiernicka
Contributing Editor: Todd McEwen
Photo Consultant: Alice Rose George
Picture Research: Lynda Marshall
Executive Editor: Pete de Bolla
US Associate Publisher: Anne Kinard, Granta, 250 West 57th
Street, Suite 1203, New York, NY 10107, USA.

Editorial and Subscription Correspondence: Granta, 44a Hobson
Street, Cambridge CB1 1NL. Telephone: (0223) 315290.
All manuscripts are welcome but must be accompanied by a
stamped, self-addressed envelope or they cannot be returned.

Subscriptions: £15.00 for four issues. Overseas add £3 postage.

Granta is photoset by Hobson Street Studio Ltd, Cambridge, and is
printed by Hazell Watson and Viney Ltd, Aylesbury, Bucks.

Granta is published by Granta Publications Ltd and distributed by
Penguin Books Ltd, Harmondsworth, Middlesex, England; Viking
Penguin Inc., 40 West 23rd St, New York, New York, USA; Penguin Books Australia Ltd, Ringwood, Victoria, Australia; Penguin
Books Canada Ltd, 2801 John Street, Markham, Ontario, Canada
L3R 1B4; Penguin Books (NZ) Ltd, 182–90 Wairau Road, Auckland 10, New Zealand. This selection copyright © 1988 by Granta
Publications Ltd.

Cover by Chris Hyde

Granta 23, Spring 1988

ISBN 014-00-8603-X

CONTENTS

· Salman Rushdie · Emma Tennant · Beryl Bainbridge · Graham Swift ·

Doris Lessing · Kazuo Ishiguro · Ian McEwan · Edna O'Brien · J.G. Ballard · Kingsley Amis · Rose Tremain ·

V.S. Pritchett · Alan Sillitoe · Elizabeth Bowen · Clive Sinclair · William Trevor · John Fowles · Jean Rhys ·

THE PENGUIN BOOK OF
MODERN BRITISH SHORT STORIES

A major new anthology in celebration of the
short story

EDITED BY
MALCOLM BRADBURY

'Thirty-four small worlds by masters of the miniature
which swell into an exhilarating portrait of the inner life
of the British since the war'
— *Mail on Sunday*

£4.95

Penguin Books

· Martin Amis · Adam Mars-Jones · Angus Wilson · William Golding ·

OBSERVATIONS

Meeting Gorbachev
Václav Havel

*T*he proposed visit by the Glasnost Tsar to the very country that is governed by those opposed to glasnost has evidently aroused many expectations. It has brought an un-precedented number of journalists to Prague. They arrive in good time; it is the Glasnost Tsar himself who keeps postponing the trip. And so the waiting newsmen occupy themselves as best they can. Dozens of them call on me; they all want to know what I think of the new Tsar. But it is embarrassing to have to keep repeating the same thoughts over and again, especially as none of them seems at all original to me: whatever I say, I am struck by the feeling that I have heard it or read it before somewhere.

Finally he arrives, and I can relax. The journalists now have something more interesting to do than listen to me telling them things they have already written.

I live near the Prague National Theatre; it's half-past nine in the evening, not a reporter in sight, so I take my dog for a walk. And what do we see? Endless rows of parked limousines and a vast number of policemen. Of course: Gorbachev is in the National Theatre watching a gala performance. Unable to resist, I make for the theatre, and thanks to my dog, who clears a path through the crowd, I manage to struggle through to the front. I stand and wait; the show must be over any minute. I look around at the people on the pavement and listen. They're just passers-by, not an organized 'rent-a-crowd', nor even people who came to catch a glimpse of Gorbachev—just nosy individuals, on their way to or from the pub or out for an evening stroll and who, like me, noticed

Photo: Patrick Aventurier (Frank Spooner)

something unusual and stopped out of curiosity. Their talk is full of sarcasm, aimed in particular at the long ranks of secret policemen, who remain impassive, obviously under orders not to do anything that might cast a shadow on Gorbachev's visit.

At long last the police suddenly come to life, the limousines' lights are switched on and their engines started, the dignitaries begin to trickle out of the theatre. And, lo and behold, there he is, Raisa at his side, plain-clothes cops swarming all around them.

Just then I have my first surprise: all these cynics, all these sarcastic wits, who just a few seconds before were making merciless fun of their rulers and their bodyguards, are suddenly transformed, as if by magic, into an enthusiastic, frenetically cheering crowd, fighting to get as near as possible to the leader-in-chief.

No: this is not about 'eternal friendship with the Soviet Union'—this is something more dangerous: these people are cheering a man who, they hope, is bringing them freedom.

I feel sad; this nation of ours never learns. How many times has it put all its faith in some external force which, it believed, would solve its problems? How many times had it ended up bitterly disillusioned, forced to admit that it could not expect help from anyone unless it was prepared, first and foremost, to help itself? And yet here we are again, making exactly the same mistake. They seem to think that Gorbachev has come to liberate them from Husák!

By now the Glasnost Tsar has reached the spot where I am standing. He is rather short and stocky, a cuddly ball-like figure hemmed in by his gigantic bodyguards, giving the impression of someone shy and helpless. On his face is what I take to be a sincere smile, and he waves to us in an almost conspiratorial way, as if greeting each and every one of us individually.

And then comes my second surprise: all of a sudden I find myself feeling sorry for him.

I try to imagine the life he must lead, all day long in the company of his hard-faced guardians, no doubt with a full agenda, endless meetings, negotiation-sessions and speeches: having to talk to a great many people; remember who is who; say witty things but at the same time make sure they are the *correct* things to say, things that the sensation-seeking outside world can't get hold of and use against him; needing always to be seen smiling and attending functions such as tonight's, when he would surely have preferred a quiet evening and a rest.

But I quickly suppress this twinge of compassion. After all, I say to myself, he has what he wants. He obviously enjoys this sort of life, or he wouldn't have chosen it in the first place. I refuse to feel sorry for him, rebuking myself for acting like all those idiots in the West who melt like snowmen in the sun as soon as some East European potentate smiles charmingly in their direction. Be realistic, I admonish myself; stick to what you've been handing out to all these foreign journalists for the last three days.

Gorbachev, the same man who here in Prague praised one of the worst governments our country has had in modern times, is walking just a few yards away from me, waving and smiling his friendly smile—and suddenly he seems to be waving and smiling at *me*.

And so to my third surprise: I realize that my sense of courtesy, compelling me to respond to a friendly greeting, works more quickly than my sense of politics, for here I am, shyly raising my arm and waving back at him.

Suddenly the small, ball-like figure disappears inside his official limousine and is driven off at a hundred kilometres an hour.

The crowd disperses slowly; people continue their journey home or to the pub, wherever it is they were going before coming across this unexpected excitement.

I walk my dog home and try to analyse my reactions.

And so to my fourth and last surprise: I don't feel the slightest regret at having given Gorbachev that shy little wave. I really don't have any reason not to return the Glasnost Tsar's greeting. It is, after all, one thing to respond to his smile, but something else again to try and excuse my own reaction by blaming him for smiling in the first place.

Translated from the Czech by George Theiner

JONATHAN RABAN
CYCLONE

I t had been raining for weeks. People had forgotten the last morning when the sky was not draped low over the roof-tops of England like a giant wash-cloth. The days were so dark that the only sign of nightfall was the slow brightening of lights in people's windows.

Rain turned the flat farm land of East Anglia into corrugated paddy fields, with standing water in every furrow. In London, people who lived in basements came home to find that their carpets had turned black with damp as the water-table rose.

Travel agents liked it. Their carousels of brochures showing places in the sun were stripped bare by customers in Barbour coats and green Wellington boots. Everyone who could find an excuse to be abroad on business was leaving the country, with the weathermen saying that they could see no change in the foreseeable future. Tomorrow, there would be more rain, with more rain moving in at the weekend. On television, there were pictures of punts afloat in village streets and men in oilskins carrying pensioners to safety. Going anywhere on the Underground was an unpredictable adventure because of flooding in the tunnels.

Then the storm came. It began as a vacuum in the atmosphere, far out over the Atlantic. Trying to fill itself, it set up a spinning mass of air, like a plug-hole sucking water from a bath; but the faster the winds blew, the more the vacuum deepened. It was an insatiable emptiness. It sucked and sucked; the air spiralled around it; the hole got bigger.

It did its best to flatten a corner of north-western France, then raced across the Channel, from the Cherbourg peninsula to the Dorset coast. Its edge was a jet stream of southerly air, weighted and thickened with moisture from the ocean. When it hit, it had the impact of a runaway truck. It made walls balloon and totter, then threw the bricks about like confetti. It lifted roofs off schools, ripped power-lines away from their pylons and let them blow free, lighting the night with flashes of St Elmo's Fire. Along the edge of the sea, it rained boats and caravans; sixty miles inland, the wind pasted windows with a grey rime of salt from the Atlantic.

The trees were still in leaf. After the many days of rain they were rooted in soft mud that released even full-grown oaks as if they were seedlings in a gardener's tray. On south-facing hillsides, whole woods were plucked out of the soil by the wind and strewn in heaps, ready for the chain-saw.

The cyclone worked its way towards the Home Counties. By two in the morning it was on the outskirts of London, where its first victim was a goat in Woking. The goat lived in a kennel, lovingly disguised by its builder as a miniature Tudor cottage, complete with half-timbering and painted thatch. The wind seized this piece of fond make-believe and tossed it skywards. No one knew for how long the goat and its cottage had been in flight, but both were found the next morning, five gardens away, with the dead goat hanged by its chain. There were several human deaths in the storm, including a tramp who was killed by a falling wall in Lincoln's Inn Fields, but the story of the flying goat gained most coverage in the popular papers.

Some people slept through the storm, mistaking the commotion for a turmoil inside themselves. They dreamed violent dreams. Others sat up through the night in dressing-gowns, making cups of tea and listening to the falling slates, the windows shaking in their frames, the oboe- and bassoon-noises of the wind as it blew down narrow streets and funnelled through the gaps between houses. Older people heard the falling trees as bombs. They huddled downstairs, waiting mutely for the first soft crump, then the flying glass, the shaking walls, the sudden entry of the open sky—but there were no wardens, no sirens; it was lonelier, more eerie than the Blitz.

No one dared go outside. You couldn't open the door against that wind, and who in his right mind would want to face the skirl of tiles, dustbins, garden furniture and plant pots? So people sat tight. In the suburbs, telephones went dead in the middle of a comforting chat with the neighbours. Electric lights dickered and snuffed out. Old candles were discovered in tool-drawers. People who cooked by electricity remembered primus stoves at the backs of cupboards. *Just so long as you can boil a kettle*, people said, *that's the main thing, isn't it?* Camping out in their houses, brewing tea, talking in low voices and listening to the wind, they surprised themselves with the cosiness of it all. At three and four in the morning, husbands and wives who'd grown as used to each other as they were to their curtains and carpets found themselves reaching for each other's nakedness.

Soon after dawn, the storm quit London, leaving a high wind blowing under a sky of bad milk. Light-headed from lack of sleep, people stared through their salt-caked windows to see cars crushed by trees and craters of muddy water in the pavements where the trees had been. Roads were strewn with tiles and broken bricks, bits of picket fencing, garden shrubs, up-ended tricycles, glass, tar-paper, fish bones, cardboard boxes. During what the radio news now called The Hurricane, everyone's rubbish had mated with everyone else's, and white stucco house fronts were curiously decorated with dribbles of gravy, tomato ketchup and raspberry yogurt.

On the Saturday morning, a day after the passage of the cyclone, Hyde Park was closed to traffic. The Carriage Road and The Ring were blocked by dozens of crashed trees, and the police had put up Danger signs on trestles to warn people away from the open craters and the trees that were still falling, slowly, their enormous roots half-in, half-out of the ground. The park was as noisy as a logging camp, and its resiny smell of sawn timber drifted deep into the city, to shoppers on Oxford Street and motorists caught in the jam on Brompton Road. There was allure in the smell alone. People felt themselves drawn to the park without quite knowing why; they ignored the warning signs; they stepped easily over the barriers of red tape that the police had strung between the trestles, and each one felt a surge of private exultation at the sight of what the storm had done.

It's so sad! people said, trying to quench their smiles—for they didn't feel sad at all. They were thrilled by the magnificent destruction of the wind: it was as if the world itself had come tumbling down, and even the shyest, most pacific people in the crowd felt some answering chord of violence in their own natures respond to this tremendous and unlooked-for act of violence in nature itself.

The sky had lifted. A meagre ration of diffused sunlight—the first for many days—lit the scene of an anarchic picnic. Children in coloured blousons swarmed in the branches of the humbled trees. Muddy dogs, tongues lolling, scrambled out of the craters. A black-and-white striped Parks Police van patrolled the bank of the Serpentine, its twin loud-hailers yawping about *risk, responsible,*

21

and *in your own best interests*; but its presence only added to the air of carnival.

Whoever you were, the wrecked landscape had something in it for you personally. For some people, it was simply an enjoyable reminder of their grace—they'd got away with it; they were survivors. They strode across the skyline of the park like generals on a battlefield after a famous victory. Others stood still, gazing, hands in pockets. Exiles, from Beirut, Kampala, Prague, Budapest, felt a proud glow of kinship with the uprooted trees. Saturday fathers, borrowing children from their one-time wives, dwelled, with a pleasure they couldn't explain to themselves, on the ragged pits in the earth, the torn turf, the canopies of exposed roots; while their children saw the park as a territory at last made fit for all-out war, and zapped their fathers with death-ray guns from behind safe jungle cover. Everyone was irrationally happier that Saturday, even the people who'd lost their roofs, who saw themselves as heroes of the hurricane and came to the park to enjoy disaster on a scale grand enough to match their own. *Isn't it sad?* they said, their voices drowned by shrilling gulls circling the trees that still survived.

BILL BRYSON
FAT GIRLS IN
DES MOINES

Bill Bryson

I come from Des Moines. Somebody had to. When you come from Des Moines you either accept the fact without question and settle down with a local girl named Bobbi and get a job at the Firestone factory and live there forever and ever, or you spend your adolescence moaning at length about what a dump it is and how you can't wait to get out, and then you settle down with a local girl named Bobbi and get a job at the Firestone factory and live there forever and ever.

Hardly anyone leaves. This is because Des Moines is the most powerful hypnotic known to man. Outside town there is a big sign that says: WELCOME TO DES MOINES. THIS IS WHAT DEATH IS LIKE. There isn't really. I just made that up. But the place does get a grip on you. People who have nothing to do with Des Moines drive in off the interstate, looking for gas or hamburgers, and stay forever. There's a New Jersey couple up the street from my parents' house whom you see wandering around from time to time looking faintly puzzled but strangely serene. Everybody in Des Moines is strangely serene.

The only person I ever knew in Des Moines who wasn't serene was Mr Piper. Mr Piper was my parents' neighbour, a leering, cherry-faced idiot who was forever getting drunk and crashing his car into telephone poles. Everywhere you went you encountered telephone poles and road signs leaning dangerously in testimony to Mr Piper's driving habits. He distributed them all over the west side of town rather in the way dogs mark trees. Mr Piper was the nearest possible human equivalent to Fred Flintstone, but less charming. He was a Shriner and a Republican—a Nixon Republican—and he appeared to feel he had a mission in life to spread offence. His favourite pastime, apart from getting drunk and crashing his car, was to get drunk and insult the neighbours, particularly us because we were Democrats, though he was prepared to insult Republicans when we weren't available.

Eventually, I grew up and moved to England. This irritated Mr Piper almost beyond measure. It was worse than being a Democrat. Whenever I was in town, Mr Piper would come over and chide me. 'I don't know what you're doing over there with all those Limeys,' he would say. 'They're not clean people.'

'Mr Piper, you don't know what you're talking about,' I would

24

Photo: Charles Harbutt (Archive)

reply in my affected British accent. 'You are a cretin.' You could talk like that to Mr Piper because (one) he *was* a cretin and (two) he never listened to anything that was said to him.

'Bobbi and I went over to London two years ago and our hotel room didn't even have a *bathroom* in it,' Mr Piper would go on. 'If you wanted to take a leak in the middle of the night you had to walk about a mile down the hallway. That isn't a clean way to live.'

'Mr Piper, the English are paragons of cleanliness. It is a well-known fact that they use more soap per capita than anyone else in Europe.'

Mr Piper would snort derisively at this. 'That doesn't mean diddly-squat, boy, just because they're cleaner than a bunch of Krauts and Eye-ties. My God, a *dog's* cleaner than a bunch of Krauts and Eye-ties. And I'll tell you something else: if his Daddy hadn't bought Illinois for him, John F. Kennedy would never have been elected President.'

I had lived around Mr Piper long enough not to be thrown by this abrupt change of tack. The theft of the 1960 presidential election was a long-standing plaint of his, one that he brought into the conversation every ten or twelve minutes regardless of the prevailing drift of the discussion. In 1963, during Kennedy's funeral, someone in the Waveland Tap punched Mr Piper in the nose for making that remark. Mr Piper was so furious that he went straight out and crashed his car into a telephone pole. Mr Piper is dead now, which is of course one thing that Des Moines prepares you for.

When I was growing up I used to think that the best thing about coming from Des Moines was that it meant you didn't come from anywhere else in Iowa. By Iowa standards, Des Moines is a Mecca of cosmopolitanism, a dynamic hub of wealth and education, where people wear three-piece suits and dark socks, often simultaneously. During the annual state high school basketball tournament, when the hayseeds from out in the state would flood into the city for a week, we used to accost them downtown and snidely offer to show them how to ride an escalator

Photo: Dennis Stock (Magnum)

or negotiate a revolving door. This wasn't always so far from reality. My friend Stan, when he was about sixteen, had to go and stay with his cousin in some remote, dusty hamlet called Dog Water or Dunceville or some such improbable spot—the kind of place where if a dog gets run over by a truck everybody goes out to have a look at it. By the second week, delirious with boredom, Stan insisted that he and his cousin drive the fifty miles into the county town, Hooterville, and find something to do. They went bowling at an alley with warped lanes and chipped balls and afterwards had a chocolate soda and looked at a *Playboy* in a drugstore, and on the way home the cousin sighed with immense satisfaction and said, 'Gee thanks, Stan. That was the best time I ever had in my whole life!' It's true.

I had to drive to Minneapolis once, and I went on a back road just to see the country. But there was nothing to see. It's just flat and hot, and full of corn and soybeans and hogs. I remember one long, shimmering stretch where I could see a couple of miles down the highway and there was a brown dot beside the road. As I got closer I saw it was a man sitting on a box by his front yard in some six-house town with a name like Spiggot or Urinal, watching my approach with inordinate interest. He watched me zip past and in the rear-view mirror I could see him still watching me going on down the road until at last I disappeared into a heat haze. The whole thing must have taken about five minutes. I wouldn't be surprised if even now he thinks of me from time to time.

He was wearing a baseball cap. You can always spot an Iowa man because he is wearing a baseball cap advertising John Deere or a feed company, and because the back of his neck has been lasered into deep crevasses by years of driving a John Deere tractor back and forth in a blazing sun. (This does not do his mind a whole lot of good either.) His other distinguishing feature is that he looks ridiculous when he takes off his shirt because his neck and arms are chocolate brown and his torso is as white as a sow's belly. In Iowa it is called a farmer's tan and it is, I believe, a badge of distinction.

Iowa women are almost always sensationally overweight—you see them at Merle Hay Mall in Des Moines on Saturdays, clammy and meaty in their shorts and halter-tops, looking a little like elephants dressed in children's clothes, yelling at their kids, calling

Photo: Dennis Stock (Magnum)

Iowa State Fair
Div. 101   Class 5.05

Single Ear

Entry No   962

Exhibitor

Raymond Goecke
Route 1
State Center, Ia.
50247

Iowa State Fair
101   Class 505

Single ear

Entry No   961

Exhibitor

Iowa State Fair
Div.   Class 505

FOURTH
PREMIUM   Ear

Entry No   967

Exhibitor

Harold Goecke
R.R. 1
State Center, Iowa

names like Dwayne and Shauna. Jack
Kerouac, of all people, thought that
Iowa women were the prettiest in the
country, but I don't think he ever went
to Merle Hay Mall on a Saturday. I will
say this, however—and it's a strange,
strange thing—the teenaged daughters
of these fat women are always utterly
delectable, as soft and gloriously
rounded and naturally fresh-smelling as
a basket of fruit. I don't know what it is
that happens to them, but it must be
awful to marry one of these nubile cuties
knowing that there is a time bomb
ticking away in her that will at some
unknown date make her bloat out into
something huge and grotesque,
presumably all of a sudden and without
much notice, like a self-inflating raft
from which the stopper has been
abruptly jerked.

Even so, I don't think I would have
stayed in Iowa. I never really felt
at home there, even when I was
small. In about 1957, my grandparents
gave me a Viewmaster for my birthday
and a packet of discs with the title
'Iowa—Our Glorious State'. I can
remember thinking, even then, that the
selection of glories was a trifle on the
thin side. With no natural features of
note, no national parks or battlefields or
famous birthplaces, the Viewmaster
people had to stretch their creative 3D
talents to the full. Putting the
Viewmaster to your eyes and clicking
the white handle gave you, as I recall, a

Photo: Dennis Stock (Magnum)

Photo on preceding two pages: Mark Godfrey (Archive)

shot of Herbert Hoover's birthplace, impressively three-dimensional, followed by Iowa's other great treasure, the Little Brown Church in the Vale (which inspired the song whose tune nobody ever quite knows), the highway bridge over the Mississippi River at Davenport (all the cars seemed to be hurrying towards Illinois), a field of waving corn, the bridge over the Missouri River at Council Bluffs and the Little Brown Church in the Vale again, taken from another angle. I can remember thinking even then that there must be more to life than that.

Then one grey Sunday afternoon when I was about ten I was watching TV and there was a documentary on about movie-making in Europe. One clip showed Anthony Perkins walking along some venerable old city street at dusk. I don't remember now if it was Rome or Paris, but the street was cobbled and shiny with rain and Perkins was hunched deep in a trench coat and I thought: 'Hey, *ç'est moi*!' I began to read—no, I began to consume—*National Geographic*s, with their pictures of glowing Lapps and mist-shrouded castles and ancient cities of infinite charm. From that moment, I wanted to be a European boy. I wanted to live in an apartment on a tree-lined street across from a park in the heart of a city, and from my bedroom window look out on a vista of hills and roof-tops. I wanted to ride trams and understand strange languages. I wanted friends named

Photo: Dennis Stock (Magnum)

Werner and Marco who wore short pants and played soccer in the street and owned toys made of wood. I cannot for the life of me think why. I wanted my mother to send me out to buy three-foot-long loaves of bread from an aromatic shop with a wooden pretzel hung above the entrance. I wanted to step outside my front door and *be* somewhere.

As soon as I was old enough I left. I left Des Moines and Iowa and the United States and the War in Vietnam and Watergate, and settled across the world. And now when I come home it is to a foreign country, full of serial murderers and sports teams in the wrong towns (the Indianapolis Colts? the Toronto Blue Jays?) and a personable old fart who is President. My mother knew that personable old fart when he was a sportscaster called Dutch Reagan at WHO Radio in Des Moines. 'He was just a nice, friendly kind of dopey guy,' my mother says.

Which, come to that, is a pretty fair description of most Iowans. Don't get me wrong. I am not for a moment suggesting that Iowans are mentally deficient. They are a decidedly intelligent and sensible people who, despite their natural conservatism, have always been prepared to elect a conscientious, clear-thinking liberal in preference to some cretinous conservative. (This used to drive

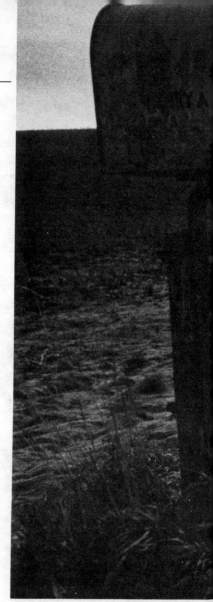

Photo: Dennis Stock (Magnum)

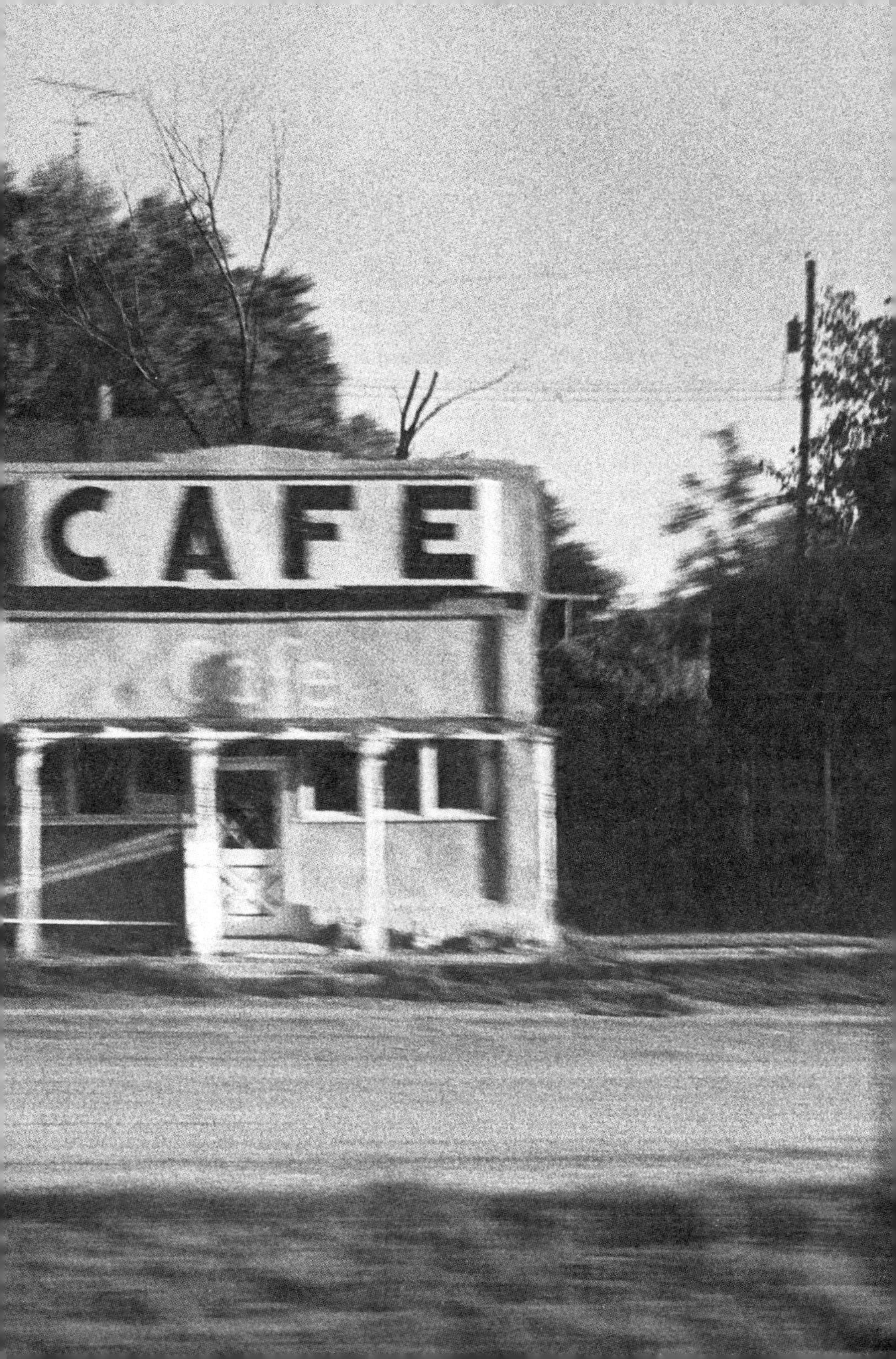
CAFE

Mr Piper practically insane.) And Iowans, I am proud to tell you, have the highest literacy rate in the nation: 99.5 per cent of grown-ups there can read. When I say they are kind of dopey, I mean that they are trusting and amiable and open. They are a tad slow, certainly—when you tell an Iowan a joke, you can see a kind of race going on between his brain and his expression—but it's not because they're incapable of high-speed mental activity, it's only that there's not much call for it. Their wits are dulled by simple, wholesome faith in God and the soil and their fellow man.

Above all, Iowans are friendly. You go into a strange diner in the south and everything goes quiet, and you realize all the other customers are looking at you as if they are sizing up the risk involved in murdering you for your wallet and leaving your body in a shallow grave somewhere out in the swamps. In Iowa you are the centre of attention, the most interesting thing to hit town since a tornado carried off old Frank Sprinkel and his tractor last May. Everybody you meet acts like he would gladly give you his last beer and let you sleep with his sister. Everyone is strangely serene.

The last time I was home, I went to Kresge's downtown and bought a bunch of postcards to send back to England. I bought the most ridiculous ones I could find—a sunset over a feedlot, a picture of farmers bravely grasping a moving staircase beside the caption: 'We rode the escalator at Merle Hay Mall!'—that sort of thing. They were so uniformly absurd that when I took them up to the check-out, I felt embarrassed by them, as if I were buying dirty magazines and hoped somehow to convey the impression that they weren't really for me. But the check-out lady regarded each of them with great interest and deliberation—just like they always do with dirty magazines, come to that.

When she looked up at me she was almost misty-eyed. She wore butterfly eyeglasses and a beehive hairdo. 'Those are real nice,' she said. 'You know, honey, I've bin in a lot of states and seen a lot of places, but I can tell you that this is just about the purtiest one I ever saw.' She really said *purtiest*. She really meant it. The poor woman was in a state of terminal hypnosis. I glanced at the cards and to my surprise I suddenly saw what she meant. I couldn't help but agree with her. They *were* purty. Together, we made a little pool of silent admiration. For one giddy, careless moment, I was almost serene myself.

Photo on preceding two pages: Richard Baron (Archive)

My father liked Iowa. He lived his whole life in the state, and indeed is even now working his way through eternity there, in Glenview Cemetery in Des Moines. But every year he became seized with a quietly maniacal urge to get out of the state and go on vacation. Every summer, without a whole lot of notice, he would load the car to groaning, hurry us into it, take off for some distant point, return to get his wallet after having driven almost to the next state, and take off again for some distant point. Every year it was the same. Every year it was awful.

The big killer was the tedium. Iowa is in the middle of the biggest plain this side of Jupiter. Climb on to a roof-top almost anywhere in the state and you are confronted with a featureless sweep of corn as far as the eye can see. It is 1,000 miles from the sea in any direction, 600 miles from the nearest mountain, 400 miles from skyscrapers and muggers and things of interest, 300 miles from people who do not habitually stick a finger in their ear and swivel it around as a preliminary to answering any question addressed to them by a stranger. To reach anywhere of even passing interest from Des Moines by car requires a journey that in other countries would be considered epic. It means days and days of unrelenting tedium, in a baking steel capsule on a ribbon of highway.

In my memory, our vacations were always taken in a big blue Rambler station wagon. It was a cruddy car—my dad always bought cruddy cars, until he got to the male menopause and started buying zippy red convertibles—but it had the great virtue of space. My sister and I in the back were yards away from my parents up front, in effect in another room. We quickly discovered during illicit forays into the picnic hamper that if you stuck a bunch of Ohio Blue Tip matches into an apple or hard-boiled egg, so that it resembled a porcupine, and casually dropped it out the back window, it was like a bomb. It would explode with a small bang and a surprisingly big flash of blue flame, causing cars following behind to veer in an amusing fashion.

My dad, miles away up front, never knew what was going on or could understand why all day long cars would zoom up alongside him with the driver gesticulating furiously, before tearing off into the distance. 'What was that all about?' he would say to my mother in a wounded tone.

'I don't know, dear,' my mother would say mildly. My mother

41

only ever said two things. She said: 'I don't know, dear.' And she said: 'Can I get you a sandwich, honey?' Occasionally on our trips she would volunteer other bits of information like 'Should that dashboard light be glowing like that, dear?' or 'I think you hit that dog/man/blind person back there, honey,' but mostly she kept quiet. This was because on vacations my father was a man obsessed. His principal obsession was trying to economize. He always took us to the crummiest hotels and motor lodges—the sort of places where there were never any coat-hangers because they had all been used by abortionists. And at the roadside eating houses, you always knew, with a sense of doom, that at some point before finishing you were going to discover someone else's congealed egg yolk lurking somewhere on your plate or plugged between the tines of your fork. This, of course, meant cooties and a long, painful death.

But even that was a relative treat. Usually we were forced to picnic by the side of the road. My father had an instinct for picking bad picnic sites—on the apron of a busy truck stop or in a little park that turned out to be in the heart of some seriously deprived ghetto so that groups of Negro children would come and stand silently by our table and watch us eating white people's foods like Hostess Cupcakes and crinkle-cut potato chips—and it always became incredibly windy the moment we stopped so that my mother spent the whole of lunchtime chasing paper plates over an area of about an acre.

In 1957 my father invested $19.98 in a gas stove that took an hour to assemble and was so wildly temperamental that we children were always ordered to stand well back when it was being lit. This always proved unnecessary, however, because the stove would flicker to life for only a few seconds before spluttering out, and my father would spend many hours turning it this way and that to keep it out of the wind, simultaneously addressing it in a low, agitated tone normally associated with the chronically insane. All the while my sister and I would implore him to take us some place with air-conditioning and linen table-cloths and ice cubes clinking in glasses of clear water. 'Dad,' we would beg, 'you're a successful man. You make a good living. Take us to a Howard Johnson's.' But he wouldn't have it. He was a child of the Depression and where capital outlays were involved he always wore the haunted look of a fugitive who has just heard bloodhounds in the distance.

Eventually, with the sun low in the sky, he would hand us hamburgers that were cold and raw and smelled of butane. We would take one bite and refuse to eat any more. So my father would lose his temper and throw everything into the car and drive us at high speed to some roadside diner where a sweaty man with a floppy hat would sling hash while grease fires danced on his grill. And afterwards, in a silent car filled with bitterness and unquenched basic needs, we would mistakenly turn off the main highway and get lost and end up in some no-hope town with a name like Draino, Indiana, or Tapwater, Missouri, and get a room in the only hotel in town, the sort of rundown place where if you wanted to watch TV it meant you had to sit in the lobby and share a cracked leatherette sofa with an old man with big sweat circles under his arms. The old man would almost certainly have only one leg and probably one other truly arresting deficiency, like no nose or a caved-in forehead, which meant that although you were sincerely intent on watching *Laramie* or *Our Miss Brooks*, you found your gaze being drawn, ineluctably and sneakily, to the amazing eaten-away body sitting beside you. You couldn't help yourself. Occasionally the man would turn out to have no tongue, in which case he would try to engage you in a lively conversation.

On another continent, 4,000 miles away, I am quietly seized with that nostalgia that overcomes you when you have reached the middle of your life and your father has recently died and it dawns on you that when he went he took a part of you with him. I want to go back to the magic places of my youth—to Mackinac Island, Estes Park, Gettysburg—and see if they were as good as I remember them. I want to hear the long, low sound of a Rock Island locomotive calling across a still night, and the clack of it receding into the distance. I want to see lightning bugs, and hear cicadas shrilling, and be inescapably immersed in that hot, crazy-making August weather that makes your underwear scoot up every crack and fissure and cling to you like latex, and drives mild-mannered men to pull out handguns in bars and light up the night with gunfire. I want to look for Ne-Hi Pop and Burma Shave signs and go to a ball game and sit at a marble-topped soda fountain and drive through the kind of small towns that Deanna Durbin and Mickey Rooney used to live in in the movies. It's time to go home.

ANTON SHAMMAS
THE RETREAT FROM
GALILEE

Grandmother Alia had never in her life heard of communism, despite the sickle laid upon her belly on Thursday, the first of April 1954. Since the early hours of that morning, Abu Jameel, the village carpenter, had been working intently in the darkness of Uncle Yusef's house across the courtyard from ours, turning the planks from an old cupboard into a coffin. His sense of humour usually covered for his slow work pace, but he was pensive and quiet now. Grandmother Alia had died the night before, and her belly puffed up, so my father had laid the iron sickle on it. Abu Jameel said something about how tiny she was, that there is no need for so much wood, and really it's a shame to waste the cupboard. From one of the leftover planks he would make a low stool on which my mother would later sit to do laundry or knead dough. I was four when Grandmother died. Only the sight of the sickle in my father's hand took my enchanted eyes from the carpenter's work. Abu Jameel winked and said, 'The old woman's fooling you—today is April the first.'

Abu Jameel was using the same table where at the end of the autumn the strings of dried tobacco were brought to be stuffed into a special, large wooden box. When they let me, I would pass the strings of tobacco already cut in two to Uncle Yusef, who would then arrange them carefully. Whenever the box filled up, Uncle Yusef and his son would lay a board over the leaves and stand on it to tamp them down. The smell of the first rain always arouses in me the smell of pressed tobacco in the small, square courtyard between our house and my uncle's, the courtyard filling up that April morning with the wailing women who had come to mourn for Grandmother as she lay there with the same clasped hands that had held this same sickle during the tobacco harvest.

Grandmother was said to have been born in the year of the Ottoman law on growing tobacco. My father did not know her birthdate. In his notebook, bound in faded leather, he calculated the date by referring to other important events in the life of her husband, Grandfather Jubran. Grandmother Alia complained all her life of the blind fate which had dumped her in the hands of the wayward Shammas family. Grandfather Jubran, who was fourteen years older, left her twice to sail far away. The first time was at the end of the last century, when he went off to Brazil for a year and left her holding Uncle Yusef, a squalling infant, in her arms. Then, on the eve of the First World War, he went to Argentina where he vanished for about ten years, leaving behind three daughters and three sons, all of them hungry. When he finally returned he brought a large wooden box and a pair of scissors. When his sons opened the box they found it was filled with rusty clothes. Grandfather Jubran had, for some reason, hidden a pair of scissors which had rusted in the box and during the three-month sea voyage had wandered among the clothes, making 'crazy patterns' as Grandmother called them. Seven years later she said goodbye to her son Jiryes, who also went to Argentina, but she would never see him again. She preserved him in her mind by telling a story about two dairy cans of milk he had once brought her, which always made her laugh so that she would have to hide her face behind her headscarf.

Letters from Uncle Jiryes, whom I never knew, would arrive from Argentina unpredictably. All of them, down to the very last one, which still lies between the pages of my father's missal, concluded, 'And to everyone who claims I have not sent him greetings, I hereby send a thousand and one greetings.' After my grandmother died, his letters were like the last signals from a sinking ship. Several months after his last one we learned from a letter sent to the village by his friend, who had accompanied him on his voyage in 1928, that he had died penniless in an old people's home. Along with enormous debts, he had left behind rumours of a local wife. This would have been in addition to his first wife, Almaza, who had never set foot on Argentinian soil, and had last seen her husband waving from the ship steaming out of Beirut harbour to take my uncle there.

Uncle Jiryes was the only one of my grandfather's sons and daughters, six in all, who inherited the 'wrinkle in the mind', as my grandmother called it, that may have been responsible for the great wanderings of the family's patriarch in the early part of the last century. From a remote village in south-west Syria, called Khabab, he eventually reached the remote village of Fassuta in Galilee, where I was destined to be born. But it seems

47

that our family's patriarch was driven there less by wanderlust than by his family's fear for his life, which was avidly sought by the Muslim clan in the village. It was Uncle Yusef who told me this, for in the early years of this century, he, like our ancestor and the other villagers of Fassuta, was also subject to persecutions and torture at the hands of the Muslim inhabitants of the nearby village of Deir El-Kasi.

Our village is built on the ruins of the Crusader castle of Fassove, which was built on the ruins of Mifshata, the Jewish village that had been settled after the destruction of the Second Temple by a group of deviant priests, and which the villagers, as a sort of Jewish-Crusader compromise, called Fassu-ta. And our ancestor took a wife there and started a family, and Grandmother Alia married Jubran, the son of that wanderer, and never managed to extinguish his passion for wandering nor that of her son Jiryes, the only one of her children to inherit that 'wrinkle of the mind'. She who marries a gypsy, as the saying goes, will learn in the end to hold the tambourine for him. But my grandmother never learned; nor did she manage, when she was nursing my Uncle Jiryes, to infuse his body with that serenity that comes from staying home. In fact it was the nursing of him that became an issue when my Uncle Jiryes decided to go off to distant Argentina. All else having failed, she told him of how much she had suffered when she nursed him, only to have given her milk in vain. My uncle calculated that the milk he had suckled from my grandmother was equal to two dairy cans. About a week before his departure he got up very early one morning, untied Uncle Yusef's donkey and set out for the village dairy. An hour later, the donkey returned alone, bearing two dairy cans of milk. My grandmother covered her face with her headscarf and said nothing.

Almaza, Uncle Jiryes's wife, was not enthusiastic about the idea of emigration. She stood on the dock in Beirut harbour and watched Uncle Jiryes's ship sail away, holding in her arms my uncle's first-born son, Anton, who was nine months old. Six months later my uncle sent her a ticket but still she wouldn't go. She remained in Beirut with some distant relatives, supporting herself by working as a cleaning woman in the homes of wealthy families. A year later word reached the village that little Anton had fallen ill and died.

At the end of the 1960s Almaza would recall that long moment on the dock. She had returned to our village, having heard that my Uncle Jiryes had begged her forgiveness in his last letter. When she walked through the village streets she held the feather pillow on which Anton had slept, even though he had been dead many years. She rented a room in a house that had, in its courtyard, a fig tree, which reminded her of the fig tree next to our house around which my uncle had tied a strip of cloth before he departed. He knew that she would stay behind, and knew that if, on his return, the cloth had become untied, it would be a sign that his wife had been unfaithful. On her visit to our village, Almaza tore her garments into strips and wound them around her arms, and begged that at her death they put only one thing into the coffin with her—Anton's pillow. I, who am writing down all these matters, was named after that child.

Tyre, Lebanon, 1938: three pretty girls looking straight at the camera. The girl on the left, Marcelle Farah, the daughter of the official in charge of the port, will marry a Frenchman who will desert her and return to his native land. The very short young lady on the right, Laurice Rizk, who has draped herself over the shoulder of the one in the middle in order to reduce the difference in height, will marry and be widowed and have no children. The girl in the centre wearing black, Elaine Bitar, will eventually be my mother.

On Friday, 30 October 1936, in my father's barbershop in the village of Fassuta, a man sat down, gave himself up to the pleasure of a shave, and with eyes closed sank into the state of total weariness which makes the mind preternaturally alert. Just as my father finished lathering the man's face, his bloodshot eyes snapped open and he looked out of the window to where three white horses stood tethered to the gate of the goat shed on the outskirts of the village. The man's hands tightened around an English rifle poised between his knees. My father, despite the presence of the rifle, kept a cool head and concentrated upon sharpening his razor on the taut leather strop. The man dozed off, but when the blade touched his sideburn, he woke with a start. From the thin cut near his ear a streak of blood unfurled. Then, stung by the alum stone my father pressed against the wound to stem the flow of blood, he again tightened his hands round the rifle and his gaze focused upon the three white horses.

Nothing was heard in the small space of the barbershop but the scratching of the razor against the beard. The man thought about the pita bread, filled with savoury *mjaddara*, that my father's nephew had been sent to bring from Grandmother Alia. Then the shadow of a figure passing the window crossed my father's hand as he drew the blade across his client's jowl, and looking out, he managed to see the hem of the dress worn by Elaine Bitar, the new teacher, who had been working in the village for the past two months at the school south of the church, where I myself would attend class twenty years later. As she walked, she dreamed about this barber she would marry, whom she had seen for the first time earlier that year in Beirut, until she ran into the *Natoor*, the village watchman and messenger, who greeted her hastily.

The *Natoor* had two things on his mind: would the *Mukhtar*, the village leader, manage to detain the British officer and his soldiers and persuade them to stay for the noon-day meal, and if so would he himself be invited to eat in the kitchen? He then hurried on to the barbershop where my father's razor had by now reached mid-chin. The *Natoor* burst in and addressed the man in the chair, cradled in the strokes of the shave. 'Khawaja Al-Asbah, the *Mukhtar* says to tell you that British soldiers have reached the village and they are looking for you.' Al-Asbah leapt up, wiped the soap off half his face, and bolted out of the door of the barbershop.

Al-Asbah, a native of Ja'ooneh, was the leader of a small group of rebels, which a year later was to fall into a British ambush near the village of Arrabeh in the lower Galilee. As he wiped the lather off half his face, he recalled the last time the British had entered his village, and how they had smashed the jars of olive oil and then slaughtered all the chickens and called it a punitive action. Al-Asbah did not wait for the return of the boy sent to bring the pitas from Grandmother Alia and who now met his little brother leaving the school. The two of them, the sons of Aunt Marie, stopped to talk with the new French teacher, and when she inquired he told her that he had been sent to bring food from Grandmother Alia's house for Al-Asbah and his two men. As the boys turned to continue on their way, the three of them heard shots from the direction of the goat shed on the outskirts of the village, and saw the three white horses fall. In the barbershop my stunned father still held the razor and gazed at the place from where Al-Asbah had gazed as he sat there, given over to the pleasures of getting shaved, and from where, if he had continued to sit there, he would have witnessed the three white horses fall.

Al-Asbah and his two companions watched their horses from a hiding-place they found inside the goat shed, and when the British soldiers burst into the shed all they found were bloodstains on the black manure. It was not until some seventeen months later, in March 1938, or so said the rumours which reached the village, that the British soldiers managed to kill Abdallah Al-Asbah near the Lebanese border. My father's nephew, meanwhile, once he saw what had happened, took the three pitas out of the cloth sack and shared them with the teacher and his little brother, and the three of them stood there chewing and heard the three last shots that put an end to the lives of the wounded horses.

Elaine Bitar would not have known that the eight-year-old boy would one day marry her daughter and that his elder brother would have his leg amputated forty years later. But those shots were to ricochet through her memory as she heard the jubilant volleys in her honour fired by the men of the village when she later returned as a bride upon a white horse, near the place called Ad-Darajeh, which means 'the terrace', near the Lebanese border early in February 1940. She was to remember those shots again two days before the Christmas of 1946, by which time she was the mother of four children.

Elias Mikha'eel had maintained a family tradition. He took leave of his senses in the fullness of his days and would run naked through the streets of the village, or else he would take his mattress out into the street and pelt it with stones, cursing it for all the hours of sleep he had wasted upon it. But the act for which he most often bobs up in the flow of the village's memory was connected with his son Nakhleh, who served in the British Police at

Tarbeekha Station. Late in 1946 the father collected all the tins which were to be filled with olive oil from the late autumn pressing. After he had cut them open and flattened them down, he explained to the fascinated onlookers that he was going to build an armoured vehicle for his son, in which he could ride safe and sound to the police station at Tarbeekha. His beloved son was murdered in his bed two days before the Christmas of 1946. The following day, during the funeral, somebody stole into our house, somehow opened the mirrored door of the cupboard, lifted the lid of the Damascene wooden box inlaid with mother-of-pearl and removed from the little blue velvet boxes all the jewellery my mother had been given as a wedding gift by her mother. My father insisted upon seeking the advice of a fortune-teller from Tarsheeha to discover the identity of the thief. In the saucer of oil on his table, my mother recognized a woman she knew, but would not say who it was. Ten years later she was to see the pearl earrings her mother had given her adorning the ears of a friend of that same woman, who came from the city in which the holy Virgin heard the news that she heard, but my mother remained silent. Just as she would remain silent four years after the theft, when my father insisted upon naming me after the child who had died in Beirut in 1929.

In 1980, I rode with my brother in his car from Haifa to Fassuta where we would take the olives to the electric press at the village of Horfeish. I had last visited this press twenty years before, in the company of my cousin Wardeh, the sister of the two boys who with my mother had watched the fall of the three white horses. It was because of the new electric press that the old press at Fassuta had declined, the press that had belonged to Abu Shacker, whose white horses would plod round and round by the light of an oil lamp. The horse turned the press-beam, which crushed the olives against the nether stone. An old man would sit there all day long, holding a can into which the olive-growers' oil would pour. And as he sat there he would pluck at his eyebrows and eyelashes and spit on the floor covered with olive husks and repeat his single unvarying curse against the Arab rebellion.

Abu Shacker, the proprietor of the olive press, was the one who, in October 1948, brought the news that the Jewish Army, the

Jaish El-Yahud, was advancing on the village. The soldiers of the *Jaish El-Inqad*, Kaukji's Arab army, had taken up positions on the hills above the village, but they were now retreating along the path that linked the village to the Northern Road. The path, which eventually would be called *Khat El-Hazeemeh*, that is, Retreater's Way, was built with the labour of many men from the nearby villages, and was intended for the passage of the Arab armies, wreathed in victory, on the day of the liberation of the homeland from the thieving Zionists.

This same way of both Victory and Retreat twisted through the eastern slopes of Tal Hlal, touched a valley also named after the same tribe and wound along the edge of the terrace called Khallet Zeinab, in memory of the woman whose life and death had inflamed the imaginations of the Galileans at the turn of the century. Folk poets spent many long nights rhyming songs in her praise. Men from all over the Galilee made their way up to Sa'sa', the village of Zeinab's birth, to behold her beauty. But the men of her village did not look kindly upon the beautiful woman, and they began to spin the web of her death. First they spread rumours about the fiery lust between Zeinab's legs and said that there was no man who could satisfy her appetite. Then they prohibited her from walking through the greening fields lest the crop withered from the rut of her lust. Finally they decided that the shame of Zeinab would pass from their village only if her passion were extinguished, and so the elders gathered one night to consider how to achieve this. At dawn several young men of the village burst into Zeinab's house, dragged her from the bed of her husband and brought her to the outskirts of the village. There they bound her hands and her feet, lifted the hem of her dress and poured gunpowder into her underpants, inserted a wick in her private parts, lit it and ran. And to this day the place is called Khallet Zeinab.

The Way of Victory, that became the Retreater's Way, meandered through these memories of the past, and then, late in October 1948, it bore the footprints of Abu Shacker, on his arrival at the village to warn the inhabitants that the soldiers of the Jews were on their way to conquer it.

Two weeks earlier Israeli planes had dropped bombs on Tarsheeha, just to the south of Fassuta, to which Al-Asbah's relatives had fled from their conquered village of Ja'ooneh. It was the season of the olive-pressing but it had been a bad year, said the olive growers. For in a bad year the olive withdraws into itself and does not attend to the sticks of the beaters and the hands of the harvesters. Also that year the olive harvesters stayed home in fear of the bombs which blurred the horizon with spirals of smoke. The inhabitants of Fassuta withdrew into their houses, or sought shelter in the church or in the caves scattered around the village. The only roosters in the village walked about in a fearful state and, at the sound of the dull explosions which shook the ground under their claws, rushed to their coops to assuage their alarm by ruffling the feathers of the hens, who clucked raucously as if they too could sense the danger in the air.

The rooster belonging to my uncle's wife would strut around the inner courtyard with lordly deliberation, taking care never to be surprised by the onset of a bombing raid. The turquoise cat would observe him, seeing what was coming, and knowing that the end, when it came, would take no account of cautionary strutting and that Death had no care in its black heart for the grief of widowed hens.

And so it came to pass that in the latter half of October my uncle's wife's rooster took leave of his senses in the face of the accumulating tension. With cockscomb erect and wattles a-tremble, he attacked the scrawny donkey who stood tied in the courtyard sunk in his own worries and suffering the pangs of hunger. The rooster spread his wings and pecked the nape of the donkey, who shook him off and kicked him with his rear legs. The turquoise cat looked on indifferently as the rooster plunged and fell near her, after having banged into the wall, and she knew she would get his head.

My uncle's wife, who came outside at the sound of the commotion, stood there at a loss, not knowing what to do first, whether to wring the rooster's neck or beat the donkey. The turquoise cat then saw my uncle's wife raining blows upon the scrawny donkey, rehearsing what was to come to pass in the near future. Then she wrung the rooster's neck and threw the head to the cat, whereupon the cat retired to her corner in the nether regions of the courtyard with her teeth sunk into the impetuous cockscomb. And the whole time the line of refugees from Tarsheeha wound along the Way of the Retreater, towards the Lebanese border.

As the Jews' army was making its way along the road winding up to Deir El-Kasi, Abu Shacker was looting its houses. The inhabitants of Deir El-Kasi had not waited for the army to arrive. They were already across the border. And Abu Shacker now entered the home of Mahmood El-Ibraheem, who had been the regional commander in the days of the Arab Rebellion. The gate to the courtyard was open, as if El-Ibraheem had just stepped out for a moment to visit a neighbour. Abu Shacker entered through the gate and stood in the courtyard, in the very spot where he had stood ten years before.

Except that then he was beaten and injured and degraded, and now he straightened his back and inhaled deeply all the smells of the house which formerly had transmitted fear and trembling. Now everything was abandoned and given unto his hand like ripe fruit. A donkey ambled along the path outside the gate, and Abu Shacker moved closer to the front door, left ajar, and pushed it gently, and with two steps was inside the house of El-Ibraheem, the man who had imposed his will upon the region during the days of the Arab Rebellion. Abu Shacker sat down on a stool and began to compose a list of all the things he wanted to take.

And then he saw a frayed sack of olives standing in the corner of the kitchen, its green olives having spilled on to the kitchen floor, their thin glistening skin seeming to be on the point of exploding from the pressure of the oil held within. This sight caused the tears held within Abu Shacker to flow down his face and he went back to the bench in the hall, plopped down on it and sobbed like the smallest of his children. The frayed sack of olives made tangible what he himself could expect within just a few hours, for his fate and the fate of Mahmood El-Ibraheem were the same.

This was the moment he saw the three jeeps and a squad of soldiers winding their way along the road on the slope of the wadi. He stood at the gate, his head empty, when a black tomcat crossed the path next to him, and instinctively he bunched his fingers

Map: Peter Covill

56

WESTERN GALILEE, 1948

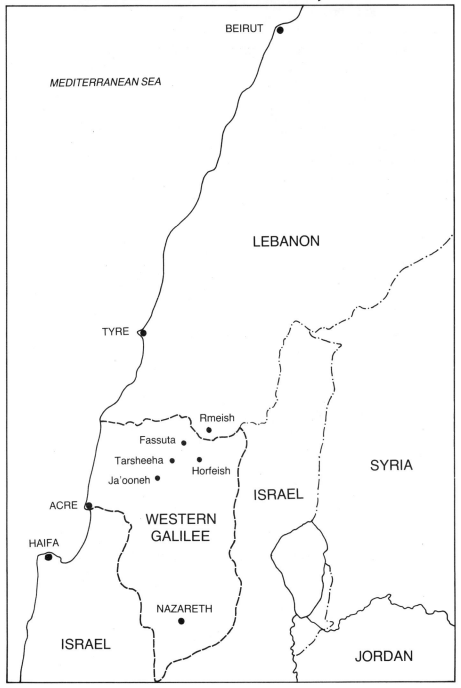

together and crossed himself. He immediately regretted having taken the Saviour's name in vain by asking him to bestow his grace upon him in the face of a black cat, and then 'the fury guttering within him flared up again because he had been wasting his time on such thoughts when the army of Jewish soldiers was coming closer and closer to him from the bottom of the wadi. Before he had managed to weigh his next moves, he turned and went back into the house, dumped out the contents of the sack which had been lying on the floor, folded it hastily and stuck it under his arm, rushed out the gate and fled for his life back to the village.

It was Saturday, 30 October 1948.

Except for Abu Shacker, all the men of the village had left at dawn for the fields surrounding the village in search of places to hide until the fury of the conqueror had passed. The women and the children took refuge in the church, and the old men, who were too frail to hide in the fields but too young to sit at home awaiting the judgements of blind Fate and too cynical to pray with the women, sat in the priest's parlour.

Abu Shacker opened the door of the priest's parlour without knocking and stood in the middle of the front room, with the jute sack still under his arm. 'What's happening?' asked my uncle. 'Couldn't be worse,' said Abu Shacker. 'They're on their way.'

The priest rose. After him the rest of the men. An ox-goad which had been prepared in advance was taken up by my uncle who walked at the head of the delegation to the eastern outskirts of the village. And when they got to Al-Mahafer my uncle took his white *kufiya* off his head and stuck the cloth onto the tip of the ox-goad, and handed the flag of surrender to the priest.

A burst of bullets was heard from the other side of the hill. The priest raised the ox-goad, and the *kufiya* fluttered in the wind. Major Nimr, who sat in the vehicle at the head of the convoy, saw it and ordered that a second burst be shot into the air. He was a Jew from this region, and knew these village elders. He also knew that there would be no resistance, and that the capitulation would be offered by a priest in black hoisting a white *kufiya*. He had already seen the delegation in his mind's eye when the convoy had gone past Tal Hlal. The inhabitants of Deir El-Kasi who were active members

of the *Jaish El-Inqad* of Kaukji had already departed on the Retreater's Way, and the new Way of the *Jaish El-Yahud* would reach its end in Fassuta before the end of the Jewish Sabbath.

The men who had fled to the fields in the morning began to gather, as the rumour reached them that the capitulation had proceeded peacefully. And thus they stood, the soldiers of the *Jaish El-Yahud* on the one side, and the inhabitants of Fassuta on the other, until from somewhere a *mijwez* was whipped out, and the men from the fields arranged themselves in a semi-circle and their feet responded as if of their own accord to the rhythm of the melody. They broke into the *Dabkeh Shamaliyeh*, a wild Galilean *dabkeh*, which had in it something of the joy of those who have been passed over by a fatal decree, and something of the pleasure of submission by the weak, and something of fawning before the stranger, and something of the canniness of the villager who draws the most unexpected weapon at the most unexpected moment. It also had in it just plain capriciousness and frivolity. One way or the other, by the time the feet tired of the dance and the capriciousness of the defeated had cooled down, all those present at the ceremony were covered with a thin white layer of dust, and, as is the way of all dust, it did not distinguish between the conquering soldier and the conquered villager. After which the official part of the ceremony began, and the celebrants were gently commanded to hand over to the army any weapons in their possession, including the ones concealed in the haystacks and the ones stashed in the fields.

The next day, after a hurried Sunday Mass, Abu Shacker stood with all the other men in front of the house of the *Mukhtar*, the village leader, where two buses were waiting, intended for an unknown destination. The commander of the Jewish Army sat on the porch of the *Mukhtar*'s house and supervised the proceedings. About two dozen men were selected by the commander and ordered to board the buses. Abu Shacker was the last of those selected. The rumours about the conduct of the *Jaish El-Yahud* left little room to doubt their fate.

The officer started his vehicle and led the two buses away. Those who remained at the *Mukhtar*'s house gazed with wet eyes after the passengers in the buses as they disappeared in clouds of dust.

The buses approached the 'church field', the spot where the road went round behind the hill and disappeared from the eye of the beholder. A small vehicle could be seen waiting there. Its driver stood next to it, his figure radiating the confidence of a man accustomed to authority. He waited for the approaching convoy, as though those who led it would help him fix whatever was wrong with his car, a blue '47 Morris. The officer gave the order to halt the convoy, descended from his vehicle, and approached the man.

'Mr Faraji,' said the officer, 'what are you doing here at a time like this?' Mr Eli Faraji, representative of Karaman Ltd, was the region's tobacco buyer, but he hadn't been seen for four weeks, most probably waiting for the village to empty itself of its inhabitants.

Mr Faraji, after the fashion of the Jews, replied to the officer's question with a question: 'And what are you doing here at a time like this?'

The officer smiled with some embarrassment. 'Following orders,' he said.

Mr Faraji looked into the first of the buses. Its passengers were familiar to him, he having more than once sat with them over a demitasse of coffee in their homes. Suddenly he saw that the whole time his hand had been poised protectively over the content of the inner pocket of the beautifully tailored jacket upon which grains of dust were now beginning to settle. With an instinctive gesture he dusted off his left shoulder, and then realized how inappropriate this gesture was for such an occasion.

He had known the officer since he was a little boy, and now as he stood before him he felt as if all the years that had passed since then had never been, and that two opposite poles were coming together right at that moment before his very eyes. The little boy he had known was leading a convoy of men doomed to wander. He wrapped his arm around the officer's shoulder with the familiarity of an old acquaintance, and the two of them disappeared behind the hill, at the edge of the 'church field'. Hopes which had withered like the threaded leaves awaiting Mr Faraji began to sprout again like the soft shoots of tobacco at the beginning of spring. The officer returned to his vehicle, and the soldier who sat next to him went over to the passengers on the buses and ordered them to return to their homes.

'God strikes with one hand and protects with the other,' murmured the elders and nodded their heads. They did not know that a second blow was to fall.

The very next day, Monday, 1 November, all the men were ordered to gather at Al-Mahafer, where they had danced the *dabkeh* of surrender. All the women crowded into the store that belonged to Uncle Nimr, my grandmother's brother. The men were ordered to stand in rows. Then a man appeared, whose head was covered with a burlap sack that had two holes for his eyes. He walked down the rows and examined the men. The first time he went along without pausing. The second time he stopped by Abu Shacker and directed his gaze at him from behind the burlap mask. Abu Shacker's heart creaked in his chest like the iron plate of his olive press that squeezed the oil from the folds of the sieves, and sweat dripped from the folds of his forehead and burned his eyes.

He recognized those eyes staring at him—he could identify them anywhere. But were his senses playing tricks on him—was this not a hallucination after sleepless nights? Was it possible that the man peering at him through the holes was Mahmood El-Ibraheem himself, the man who had been the regional commander in the days of the Rebellion twelve years before and was now one of the commanders of Kaukji's *Jaish El-Inqad* which had taken the Retreater's Way only a few days ago? He had been sure that these awful times would leave him unscathed, and that he would no longer be subject to the torments of Mahmood El-Ibraheem and his men. But now, as in a nightmare, this famous rebel and military commander had turned his coat like a burlap sack and handed over to the *Jaish El-Yahud* people whom he indicated as having collaborated with Kaukji's army. But why should Mahmood El-Ibraheem, if indeed it was him, pause by Abu Shacker, who has given support neither to the Arab Rebellion nor to the rescuing army? The seconds stretch out, and his nerves stretch and his knees shake more than they ever have in his entire life. And then the burlap head continued on his way and, passing quickly through the rows, he went over to the officer and shook his head.

Once the man and the soldiers had climbed into their vehicles and departed for their headquarters in Deir El-Kasi, the village which would eventually be called Elkosh, all the men crowded around Abu Shacker. They rejoiced with him in his deliverance when he seemed so close to the edge. But even more they wanted to know why the burlap head had apparently chosen him, of all Allah's creatures, and afterwards changed his mind. What had Abu Shacker done in secret? What had he wrought on the Army of the Jews?

But soon they began to shake their heads in pity, for Abu Shacker was the man who ten years earlier had been cruelly beaten by the rebels who suspected him of collaborating with the British, and ever since he had been peculiar and was said to have visions. For now he swore by all he holds dear that the man behind the burlap was none other than Mahmood El-Ibraheem, for whose head in a burlap bag both the British and the Jews had offered substantial rewards. Even though the villagers had no particular affection for this El-Ibraheem, and had suffered at his hands, there was nevertheless a limit to fantasy—to accuse him of collaborating with the Jews that he hated! 'There is no way, Abu Shacker.' But Abu Shacker insisted.

That night he could not sleep. In the early hours he slipped away to the olive press where he retrieved his famous pistol, which he had hidden in the shaft of the grindstone, and tied it around his waist with a rope.

At daybreak rumours fluttered their wings noisily through the village.

There were those who said that a patrol of Jewish soldiers had heard a shot from the direction of the abandoned house of Mahmood El-Ibraheem in Deir El-Kasi. When they rushed there they saw Abu Shacker standing at the gate with his pistol in his hand, and hanging on the iron pole in the front of the house was the body of Mahmood El-Ibraheem swinging back and forth. On his chest rustled a sheet of paper upon which was written 'Thus Shall Be Done to Traitors'.

There were those who said that the Jews suspected Abu Shacker of having executed Mahmood El-Ibraheem for collaborating with them.

And there were also those who said that it was the Jews who had hanged him once they had got what they wanted from him.

Abu Shacker was held for a week. On his return, his lips were sealed, and after the fashion of village rumours, those about Abu Shacker soon flew away. The villagers didn't know that another day of reckoning was yet to come.

On Monday, 15 November, my mother stood in the kitchen preparing stuffed tripe. It was the custom of our family to have stuffed tripe for dinner on Mondays if we had been lucky enough to acquire the entrails of a goat which had been slaughtered the previous day at the butcher's. If it had not been for the tripe it is doubtful that my mother would have remembered that day and its events.

Grandmother Alia was, at that moment, on her way to the home of Aunt Jaleeleh in the centre of the village, and she'd just walked past my father's shop, bent her head wrapped in its black scarf, made blinkers of her hands (the better to see in through the window pane), greeted my father who was deep in his work and continued on her way.

Aunt Jaleeleh stood in the doorway to her house, her apron dangling from her hand and her mouth open wide in shock. She had just been told the rumour that the axe had fallen and that the commander stationed in Deir El-Kasi had ordered that all the inhabitants of Fassuta must abandon their village that day before sunset.

Grandmother Alia covered her face with the edge of her headscarf and turned on her heel without a word and went to tell my father. As they hurried through the courtyard to our house the starving donkey threw a weary bray at them, knowing that it wasn't from them that his next meal would come. When my father reached the kitchen door he told my mother to leave the tripe. The turquoise cat began to rub against his legs, and he took the tripe from the table and threw it all to the cat, silencing my mother's protests as he explained the situation to her. The seams of the blanket and pillow covers were quickly opened and stuffed with whatever we could carry on the road. My father took down the jar strictly reserved for very important guests—in which white balls of *labaneh* cheese were preserved in the purest olive oil—pulled out a pile of wafer-thin bread from the copper basin, and then spread the *labaneh* over each piece, rolling it in the shape of a sceptre—'*labaneh* brides' for the road.

Suddenly all eyes turned upon the gaunt donkey who stood there patiently, as donkeys do, in the courtyard of the house. For he was now to lead the refugees to a safe haven and carry their worldly goods. From its hiding place in the stable, my uncle's wife took a full measure of barley, which had been put away for an emergency like this, brought out the dough basin, laid it before the donkey and poured the barley into it. With a full-hearted curse, she commanded the starving donkey, who for long months had not tasted barley, to eat to his heart's content. The donkey stared as if he couldn't believe his eyes, flared his nostrils, and prepared for a miraculous feast. The turquoise cat paused a moment in the relishing of her tripe, looked alternately at my uncle's wife and at the donkey, and with feline wisdom went back to her own last supper.

The village priest meanwhile had gone to appear before the commander in Deir El-Kasi to speak to his heart and persuade him to rescind the terrible decree. When he returned, the *Mukhtar* who was waiting for him at the outskirts of the village was shocked by the exorbitance of the ransom demanded—forty pounds. In the village at that time there were only the twenty pounds which had been in the inside pocket of the jacket of the tobacco buyer, Eli Faraji. And even if you were to search with an oil lamp and a wick, as the villagers say, you wouldn't find more than perhaps a few additional pounds. But these had been hidden inside pillows for even worse occasions than this, when all other alternatives might be sealed off, and the owners of these pounds would rather wander to the ends of the earth than hand them over to a rapacious officer. Therefore they set out for the village of Rmeish on the other side of the border to hire camels for the journey.

Again the priest went forth and came before the commander. He laid an envelope on the table and said to him: 'That's all there is.' The commander was sufficiently softened by the twenty pounds not to banish the inhabitants from their village. A message was sent to those in Rmeish that the decree was annulled. The mattresses and the pillows and the quilts were returned to their covers.

But by the time the message reached my uncle's wife it was too late. She ran to the basin to rescue what was left of the precious barley. The basin gleamed in the twilight, the donkey still snuffling at the bottom in case a grain or two remained. My uncle's wife went to the stable and took a stick. She went back to the voracious donkey and began to beat him, first with blows of rage because the family's supply of barley was gone, then with blows of anger at herself for having rushed to pay the beast for work he hadn't done, and finally with blows of stifled sobbing because of the Arabs and the Jews and the rebels and the soldiers and the wars and the refugees and pitiless Fate and poverty and her bellyful of it all, and especially because she wanted to stop beating him and couldn't.

And then winter came as a complete surprise, as if it had waited for the war to pass over our village and for peace and quiet to return to our homes, before sending down upon us its own lightning and thunder. But the world did not return to its previous state, for the order of things was disturbed. The bird that my uncle called the *tatamus*, who would come to the village from the cold fields and seek out warm nooks in the walls of the houses, so that my uncle would know that the snow was on its way— this time the *tatamus* came to the village even though the cold edge of approaching snow was not yet in the air. The fireflies whose twinkling lit up the summer nights invaded the village out of season and gathered at the entrance of Abu Shacker's olive press, to which were brought the sacks of olives for the pressing that had been delayed.

Abu Shacker, who was still keeping his mouth shut, watched the fireflies and turned over his memories of the events of that night in Mahmood El-Ibraheem's house. Again and again he saw himself drawing his pistol and firing at the cigarette flashing in the darkness, and by the time he realized that it was nothing but a firefly the soldiers of the *Jaish El-Yahud* had grabbed him and were taking him to their commander. And behind him, under the cover of darkness, swung the body which just a moment ago had kicked away the bench, and fluttered with the last gasps of one who could not bear the humiliation of exile and the shame of wandering.

The face floated up into the pale light of a lone firefly and sank down again into darkness.

Translated from the Hebrew by Vivian Eden

FAWWAZ TRABOULSI
A GUIDE TO THE
CITY OF BEIRUT

Archaeology

These are the ruins of Beirut: the Ottoman Beirut, the Arab Beirut, the Roman Beirut, the Hellenic Beirut, the Phoenician Beirut. The Beirut today. *Beirut*: the word means *well*. In Beirut, a well reveals layer upon layer, generation after generation, of ruins.

Experimentation

You will find the following in Beirut:

1. The semi-nuclear bomb.
2. The smart bomb.
3. The laser-guided bomb.
4. The implosion bomb.
5. The cluster bomb.
6. The fragmentation bomb.
7. The concussion bomb.
8. The phosphorus bomb.

Beirut is a city of technological experiment.

Quotes

Abou Ali Iyad, a Palestian leader, in the forests of Ajloun in Jordan: 'Better to die on our feet than live on our knees.'

Dolores Ibaruri, wife of a Spanish miner, in Guernica: 'Better to die on our feet than live on our knees.'

Metal

The Cluster Bomb.

Type: The MK 118 anti-vehicle/anti-personnel Bomb.

Each cluster bomb dispenses, upon fragmentation, approximately 200,000 shrapnels.

The injury: The wounds are neat-looking, like a cigarette burn or a slither: they don't look so bad. But because of the velocity, they fracture and splinter the bone, chewing up the tissue and the nerves and the veins, so that a doctor has no choice: he has to cut the injured limbs off; there's no way to make a repair.

The treatment: fifty per cent of all victims of the cluster bomb undergo amputation surgery. It was named by surgeons, operating in Beirut in the summer of 1982, the Begin amputation, after the Israeli Prime Minister.

Metal

The Phosphorus Bomb.

Characteristics: an incendiary bomb that melts and distorts metal.

Injuries: two quotes.

> Phosphorus sticks to the skin and can burn for hours. It cannot be extinguished by water, which causes a chemical reaction that makes the wound burn more.

> It would hit a large part of the body—and can go inside the deepest human body—and the whole body would be transformed to black. Not red. The colour of the skin would be black, dark.

Description of a case: 'His foot was burned off and the exposed cartilage was still smouldering. When his nose was pinched, puffs of smoke appeared from his lungs. He was burning inside for six hours. He will not survive.'

Treatment: The Begin amputation.

Quotes

Menachem Begin, Lebanon, 1982: 'I am ready to kill ten Lebanese civilians and five Palestinians if this leads to the elimination of a single Palestinian *fidai.*'

General Molla, Spain, 1937: 'I will not hesitate, if necessary, to kill half the Spanish people in order to achieve victory.'

Descriptions of the effects of cluster and phosphorus bombs cited from *Israel in Lebanon, The Report of the International Commission to inquire into reported Violations of International Law by Israel during its Invasion of the Lebanon,* Macbride et al. 'A Guide' is based on a text translated from the Arabic by John Berger and Fawwaz Traboulsi.

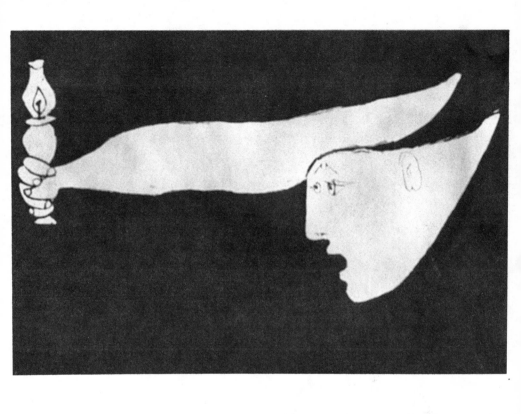

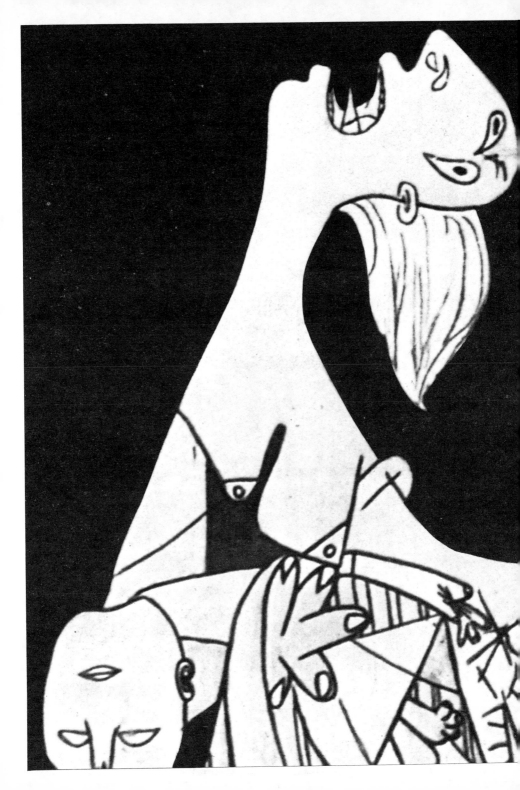

Guernica courtesy of The Prado, Madrid

MARTHA
GELLHORN
THE THIRTIES

M y life began in February 1930. I got ready in the summer of 1929, by leaving college at the end of my junior year, against my father's will, and running through two jobs, proof that I could make my way and pay for it if I didn't mind a diet of doughnuts and pawning my typewriter to tide me over weekends. 1930 was the real thing. I persuaded the Holland America Line to give me free passage in steerage, then described as Student Third Class, in return for a glowing article to use in their trade magazine. Aged twenty-one, with a suitcase and about seventy-five dollars, I set off for Paris, where I knew nobody—a joyful confident grain of sand in a vast rising sandstorm. I had visited Paris twice before and it was not my dream city, but I intended to become a foreign correspondent within a few weeks, and Paris was the obvious place to launch my career.

The launch lacked a certain *savoir-faire*. The flower stalls at the Place de la Madeleine suited my liking for a pretty neighbourhood. On a nearby side-street I found a hotel, no more than a doorway, a desk and dark stairs, and was gratified by the price of the room. The room was smelly and squalid and I thought it impractical to have a mirror on the ceiling but perhaps that was a French custom. There was an amazing amount of noise in the corridors and other rooms but perhaps the French did a lot of roaming in hotels. I could not understand why the man at the desk grew more unfriendly each time he saw me, when I was probably the friendliest person in Paris.

Having checked the telephone directory, I presented myself at the office of the *New York Times* and informed the bureau chief, a lovely elderly Englishman aged maybe forty, that I was prepared to start work as a foreign correspondent on his staff. He had been smiling hugely at my opening remarks and mopped up tears of laughter when he learned where I lived. He took me to lunch—my enthusiasm for free meals was unbounded—and explained that I was staying in a *maison de passe,* where rooms were rented by the hour to erotic couples. My new English friend insisted that I change my address, and bribed me with an invitation to report next week again at lunch. He suggested the Left Bank; I would be safer in the students' milieu.

The private life of the French was their own business and no inconvenience to me, but I was offended by the unfriendliness of the man at the hotel desk. I got off the *Métro* at Saint Germain des Prés, thinking it would be nice to live in fields if not near flowers, and was sorry to find no fields but did find a charming little hotel on the rue de l'Université, which no doubt meant a street for students. This hotel was also cheap, and a grand piano, with a big vase of flowers on it, filled the tiny foyer. My windowless room had a glass door opening onto an iron runway. The bath, at extra cost, was four flights down in the courtyard. I thought it remarkable that young men, the other residents, cried so much and quarrelled in such screeching voices, but I liked the way they played Chopin on the grand piano and kept fresh flowers in the big vase.

An ex-Princetonian, studying at the Beaux Arts, a throw-back to my college days, came to collect me for dinner one night and was ardently approached by a Chopin pianist, and scandalized. He explained homosexuality, since I had never heard of it. I pointed out that I could hardly be safer than in a homosexual hotel and, besides, I was sick of people butting in on my living arrangements. I won and lost jobs without surprise and saved up, from my nothing earnings, so that I could eat the least expensive dish at a Russian restaurant where I mooned with silent love for a glorious White Russian balalaika player.

The years in France and adjacent countries were never easy, never dull and an education at last. Unlike the gifted Americans and British who settled in Paris in the twenties and lived among each other in what seems to me a cosy literary world, I soon lived entirely among the French, not a cosy world. The men were politicians and political journalists; the students of my generation were just as fervently political. Money depended on age; the old had it, some of them had lashings of it; the young did not.

I was astonished, a few years later in England, to meet young men who neither worked nor intended to work and were apparently rich. A combination of the English eldest son syndrome and the time-honoured method of living on debts, charm and hospitality. They were much more fun than the French, but I thought them half-witted; they knew nothing about real life. Real life was the terrible

English mill towns, the terrible mining towns in northern France, slums, strikes, protest marches broken up by the mounted Garde Républicaine, frantic underpaid workers and frantic half-starved unemployed. Real life was the Have-nots.

The Haves were sometimes enjoyable, generally ornamental and a valuable source of free meals and country visits. I did not recognize the power of the Haves. Because of my own poverty, fretting over centimes, make-do or do-without, keeping up my appearance on half a shoe-string, I absorbed a sense of what true poverty means, the kind you never chose and cannot escape, the prison of it. Maybe that was the most useful part of my education. It was a very high-class education, all in all, standing room at ground level to watch history as it happened.

During the French years, I returned to America once in 1931. This period is lost in the mists of time. I know that I travelled a lot and began the stumbling, interminable work on my first novel. (When it finally appeared, in 1934, my father read it and said, rightly, that he could not understand why anyone had published it. I have, also rightly, obliterated it ever since.) With a French companion in the autumn of 1931, I made a long hardship journey across the continent from the east to the west coast. It was all new and exotic to him, not to me, and I remember very little.

Suddenly, one sunny morning in London in 1936, I was to remember a lynching in Mississippi, and 'Justice At Night' wrote itself as if by Ouija board. I was cadging bed and breakfast from H. G. Wells; cadging room from those who had it was a major occupation of the moneyless young in those days. Wells nagged steadily about my writing habits; a professional writer had to work every morning for a fixed number of hours, as he did. Not me. I dug in solitude like a feverish mole until I had dug through to the end, then emerged into daylight, carefree, ready for anything except my typewriter; until the next time. I had just finished my book on the unemployed, *The Trouble I've Seen*, and spent the London nights dancing with young gentlemen of my acquaintance and was not about to adopt Wells's nine-thirty a.m. to twelve-thirty p.m. regime. Not then or ever. That morning, to show him I could write if I felt like it, I sat in his garden and let 'Justice at Night' produce itself. Wells sent it to the *Spectator*. I had already moved on to

Germany where I ceased being a pacifist and became an ardent anti-Fascist.

L ate in 1934, in Paris, it dawned on me that my own country was in trouble. I thought that trouble was a European speciality. America was safe, rich and quiet, separate from the life around me. Upon finally realizing my mistake, I decided to return and offer my services to the nation. Which I did on a miserable little tub of the Bernstein Line, price of passage eighty-five dollars; arriving in New York on 10 October. By 16 October I was enrolled in the service of the nation.

In Washington, a reporter friend introduced me to Harry Hopkins, who was then the Director of the Federal Emergency Relief Administration, the FERA, the first national American dole. Mr Hopkins was hiring a few people to travel around the country and report back to him on how FERA worked in practice. I told Mr Hopkins that I knew a lot about unemployment and was a seasoned reporter; the first was true enough, the second not. I had been writing anything I could for any money I could earn, and the childish first novel; scarcely star-rating. I think I remember a smiling blue gleam in Mr Hopkins's eyes at that interview.

I wore the only clothes I had, a Schiaparelli suit in nubbly brown tweed fastened up to its Chinese collar with large brown leather clips, and Schiap's version of an Anzac hat in brown crochet work adorned by a spike of cock-pheasant feathers. I could not afford to buy clothes in the ordinary way and dressed myself in *soldes*, the bargain discarded outfits that the models of the great couturiers had worn in their last collections. Also I painted my face like the Parisian ladies, lots of eye-shadow, mascara and lipstick, which was not at all the style for American ladies then and certainly not for social workers in federal employment. Mr Hopkins may have been entertaining himself. He could sack me at any moment and was not delving deep into the public purse, though to me the job meant untold riches: seventy-five dollars a week, train vouchers and five dollars per diem travel allowance for food and hotels.

For three weeks short of a year, I crossed the country, south, north, east, midwest, far west, wrote innumerable reports and kept no copies, the chronic bad habit of my professional life. A few years ago, someone found six of my early reports in Mrs Roosevelt's papers at the Hyde Park Roosevelt Library. I have cut and stuck three together because I think they are a small but vital record of a period in American history. They were not written for publication, they can hardly be called written; banged out in haste as information.

After a few months, I was so outraged by the wretched treatment of the unemployed that I stormed back to Washington and announced to Mr Hopkins that I was resigning to write a bitter exposé of the misery I had seen. I did not pause to reflect that I had no newspaper or magazine contacts and was unlikely to create a nationwide outcry of moral indignation. Instead of telling me not to waste his time, Mr Hopkins urged me to talk to Mrs Roosevelt before resigning; he had sent her my reports. I walked over to the White House, feeling grumpy and grudging. Mrs Roosevelt, who listened to everyone with care, listened to my tirade and said, 'You should talk to Franklin.'

That night I was invited to dinner at the White House, seated next to the President in my black sweater and skirt (by then I was rich enough to buy ordinary clothes), and observed in glum silence the white and gold china and the copious though not gourmet food, hating this table full of cheerful well-fed guests in evening clothes. Didn't they know that better people were barefoot and in rags and half-starved; didn't they know anything about America?

Mrs Roosevelt, being somewhat deaf, had a high sharp voice when talking loudly. She rose at the far end of the table and shouted, 'Franklin, talk to that girl. She says all the unemployed have pellagra and syphilis.' This silenced the table for an instant, followed by an explosion of laughter; I was ready to get up and go. The President hid his amusement, listened to the little I was willing to say—not much, suffocated by anger—and asked me to come and see him again. In that quaint way, my friendship with the Roosevelts began and lasted the rest of their lives. Mrs Roosevelt persuaded me that I could help the unemployed more by sticking to the job, so I went back to work until I was fired, courtesy of the FBI.

I think I know what happened now, though I had a more grandiose explanation at the time. In a little town on a lake in Idaho called Coeur d'Alene, pronounced Cur Daleen, I found the unemployed victimized as often before by a crooked contractor. These men, who had all been small farmers or ranchers on their own land, shovelled dirt from here to there until the contractor collected the shovels, threw them in the lake and pocketed a tidy commission on an order for new shovels. Meantime the men were idle, unpaid and had to endure a humiliating means-test for direct dole money to see them through.

I had never understood the frequent queries from Washington about 'protest groups'. I thought Washington was idiotic—they didn't realize that these people suffered from despair, not anger. But I was angry. By buying them beer and haranguing them, I convinced a few hesitant men to break the windows of the FERA office at night. Afterwards someone would surely come and look into their grievances. Then I moved on to the next stop, Seattle, while the FBI showed up at speed in Coeur d'Alene, alarmed by that first puny act of violence. Naturally the men told the FBI that the Relief lady had suggested this good idea; the contractor was arrested for fraud, they got their shovels for keeps, and I was recalled to Washington.

I wrote to my parents jubilantly and conceitedly: 'I'm out of this man's government because I'm a "dangerous Communist" and the Department of Justice believes me to be subversive and a menace. Isn't it flattering? I shrieked with laughter when Aubrey [Williams, Mr Hopkins's deputy] told me; seems the unemployed go about quoting me and refuse—after my visits—to take things lying down.'

While I was collecting bits and pieces from my seldom-used desk in the Washington FERA office, the President's secretary rang with a message from the President. He and Mrs Roosevelt, who was out of town, had heard that I was dismissed and were worried about my finances because I would not find another government job with the FBI scowling, so they felt it would be best if I lived at the White House until I sorted myself out. I thought this was kind and helpful but did not see it as extraordinary—a cameo example of the way the Roosevelts serenely made their own choices and judgements.

Everyone in the FERA office was outdone by the stupid interfering FBI; I treated the whole thing as a joke. Naturally the Roosevelts, the most intelligent people in the country, knew it was all nonsense, though, being the older generation, they considered the practical side. I had saved enough money for time to write a book, but had not planned where to work and the White House would be a good quiet place to start. It was, too, but I needed the complete mole existence for writing and departed from the White House with thanks and kisses as soon as a friend offered me his empty remote house in Connecticut. Being fired was an honourable discharge in my view, not like quitting; and I was very happy to work on fiction again. When I finished the book, I went back to Europe, having done my duty by my country.

That was the time when I really loved my compatriots, 'the insulted and injured', Americans I had never known before. It was the only time that I have fully trusted and respected the American Presidency and its influence on the government and the people. Now it is accepted that Franklin Roosevelt was one of the rare great Presidents. While he was in office, until America entered the war, both the Roosevelts were daily vilified and mocked in the Republican press, and both were indifferent to these attacks. Mrs Roosevelt was in herself a moral true north. I think the President's own affliction—he was crippled by polio at the age of thirty-nine—taught him sympathy for misfortune. They were wise. They had natural dignity and no need or liking for the panoply of power. I miss above all their private and public fearlessness.

Born to every privilege that America can offer, they were neither impressed by privilege nor interested in placating it. The New Deal, the Roosevelt regime, was truly geared to concern for the majority of the citizens. I am very glad that I grew up in America when I did and glad that I knew it when the Roosevelts lived in the White House. Superpower America is another country.

I went to Spain in March 1937 and became a war correspondent by accident. From then on, until 1947, I wrote no journalism except war reports, apart from four articles in 1938. *Collier's*, my employer, cabled me in Barcelona asking me to go to Prague. In war, I never knew anything beyond what I could see and hear, a full-time occupation. The Big Picture always exists, and I seem to have spent my life observing how desperately the Big Picture affects the little people who did not devise it and have no control over it. I didn't know what was happening around Madrid and certainly not what was happening in Czechoslovakia but now I had suddenly at long last become a foreign correspondent.

I went to Czechoslovakia when the Czechs were mobilized and determined to fight for their country against Hitler; I went the second time after the Munich Pact. In between, at *Collier's* request, I went to England, because my editor wanted some idea of the English reaction to oncoming war. I had already done a similar article about France. I found the mental climate in England intolerable; sodden imagination, no distress for others beyond the sceptr'd isle.

Three days before he flew to Berchtesgaden to sign away the life of Czechoslovakia, the Prime Minister, Neville Chamberlain, a stick figure with a fossil mind, addressed the nation by radio, speaking to and for the meanest stupidity of his people: 'How horrible, fantastic, incredible it is that we should be digging trenches and trying on gas masks because of a quarrel in a far-away country between people of whom we know nothing.' Then he came back from Germany, waving that shameful piece of paper and proclaiming 'peace with honour' to the cheering crowds. This same government had starved the Republic of Spain through its nefarious Non-Intervention Treaty, while Hitler and Mussolini were free to aid Franco. I thought the only good British were in the International Brigade in Spain; I was finished with England, would never set foot again in the miserable self-centred country. Instead of which, since 1943, London has been the one fixed point in my nomadic life.

At the end of the decade, in December 1939, I was again in Paris on my way home to Cuba from the Russo-Finnish War. Czechoslovakia and Spain were lost and I knew I was saying goodbye to Europe. I did not think it was a phoney war; I thought it would be a hell-on-earth war and a long one. Having started off in this city, so merry and so ignorant almost ten years before, here I was despairing for Europe and broken-hearted for Spain. The powers of evil and money ruled the world.

Now brave men and women, anti-Fascists all over Europe, would be prey for the Gestapo. I had not then taken in the destiny planned for the Jews. Perhaps this was because in Germany in the summer of 1936 there were no startling signs of persecution, not when Nazi Germany was host to the Olympic Games, and on its best behaviour. I was obsessed by what Hitler was doing outside his country, not inside Germany. To me, Jews and anti-Fascists were the same, caught in the same trap, equally condemned. Passports were the only escape. None of the people I knew and cared for had passports, or anywhere to run. I saw them all as waiting for a sure death sentence, unsure of the date of execution.

Paris was beautiful and peaceful in the snow, peacefully empty. Men I had known in the early thirties, now important people, ate in grand restaurants and told me not to be so sad and foreboding. Cheer up, we have the Maginot Line. I owned an invaluable green American passport. I was perfectly safe; I even had some money in the bank because *Collier's* paid generously. I felt like a profiteer, ashamed and useless. By geographical chance, the piece of the map where I was born, I could walk away. I had the great unfair advantage of choice.

I think I learned the last lesson of those educational years unconsciously. I had witnessed every kind of bravery in lives condemned by poverty and condemned by war; I had seen how others died. I got a measure for my own life; whatever its trials and tribulations, they would always be petty insignificant stuff by comparison.

Washington, DC
11 November 1934

My Dear Mr Hopkins,

I came in today from Gastonia, North Carolina, and
was as flat and grim as is to be expected. I got a notice
from your office asking about 'protest groups'. All
during this trip in both Carolinas I have been thinking to
myself about that curious phrase 'red menace', and
wondering where said menace hid itself. Every house I
visited—mill worker or unemployed—had a picture of
the President. These ranged from newspaper clippings
(in destitute homes) to large coloured prints, framed in
gilt cardboard. The portrait holds the place of honour
over the mantel; I can only compare this to the Italian
peasant's Madonna. I have seen people who, according
to any standard, have practically nothing in life and
practically nothing to look forward to or hope for. But
there is hope, confidence, something intangible and
real: 'The President isn't going to forget us.'

I went to see a woman with five children who was
living on relief ($3.40 a week). Her picture of the
President was a small one. Her children have no shoes
and the woman is terrified of the coming cold. There is
almost no furniture left in the home, and you can
imagine what and how they eat. But she said, suddenly
brightening, 'I'd give my heart to see the President. I
know he means to do everything he can for us, but they
make it hard for him; they won't let him.'

In many mill villages, evictions have been served;
more threatened. These men are in a terrible fix. (Lord,
how barren the language seems: these men are faced by
the prospect of hunger and cold and homelessness and of
becoming dependent beggars—in their own eyes. What
more a man can face, I don't know.) You would expect
to find them maddened with fear, with hostility. I

expected and waited for 'lawless' talk, threats, or at least blank despair. And I didn't find it. I found a kind of contained and quiet misery; fear for their families and fear that their children wouldn't be able to go to school. What is keeping them sane, keeping them going on and hoping, is their belief in the President.

Boston, Massachusetts
26 November 1934

My Dear Mr Hopkins,

It seems that our [relief] administrators are frequently hired on the recommendations of the Mayor and the Board of Aldermen. The administrator is a nice inefficient guy who is being rewarded for being somebody's cousin. The direct relief is handled by the Public Welfare which is a municipal biz and purely political in personnel. I can't very well let myself go about the quality of these administrators; they are criminally incompetent.

In one town the [relief] investigators (who are supposed to be doing some social work) are members of the Vice Squad who have been loaned for the job. Usually there is only one investigation at the office (followed by a perfunctory home visit) to establish the eligibility of the client for relief. I can't see that these questions do anything except hurt and offend the unemployed, destroy his pride, make him feel that he has sunk into a pauperized substrata.

I think this is a wretched job; wretched in every way. Politics is bad enough in any shape; but it shouldn't get around to manhandling the destitute.

I could go on and on. It is hard to believe that these conditions exist in a civilized country. I have been going into homes at mealtimes and seeing what they eat. It isn't possible; it isn't enough to begin with and then every article of food is calculated to destroy health. But how can they help that; if you're hungry you eat 'to fill up—but the kids ain't getting what's right for them; they're pale and thin. I can't do anything about it and sometimes I just wish we were all dead.'

I'm not thrilled with Massachusetts.

Camden, New Jersey
25 April 1935

My Dear Mr Hopkins,

I have spent a week in Camden. It surprises me to find how radically attitudes can change within four or five months. Times were of course lousy, but you had faith in the President and the New Deal and things would surely pick up. This, as I wrote you then, hung on an almost mystic belief in Mr Roosevelt, a combination of wishful thinking and great personal loyalty.

In this town, and I believe it is a typical eastern industrial city, the unemployed are as despairing a crew as I have ever seen. Young men say, 'We'll never find work.' Men over forty say, 'Even if there was any work we wouldn't get it; we're too old.' They have been on relief too long; this is like the third year of the war when everything peters out into grey resignation. Moreover they are no longer sustained by confidence in the President.

At one big meeting I attended the high point of the

evening was a prize drawing: chances were a penny apiece and the prizes were food: a chicken, a duck, four cans of something, and a bushel of potatoes. At the risk of seeming slobbery, I must say it was one of the most forlorn and pitiful things I have ever seen in my life. These people had somehow collected a few pennies. They waited with passionate eagerness while the chances were read out, to see if they were going to be able to take some food home to the family. The man who won the duck said, 'No, we won't eat it, my little girl has been asking for a bunny for Easter and maybe she can make a pet of the duck. She hasn't got anything else to play with.'

I had a revealing talk with the local president of the Union, an American (most of the labour here is Italian, Polish or very illiterate Negro). He is a superior kind of man, intelligent, cynical, calm. He has of course been laid off. He says that the speed with which workers become demoralized is amazing. He expects that his own Union cohorts will stay in the Union for a few months and then drift into unemployed Councils or Leagues. He says also that it's terrible to see how quickly they let everything slide; it takes about three months for a man to get dirty, to stop caring about how his home looks, to get lazy and demoralized and (he suspects) unable to work.

This matter—the demoralization point—has interested me; I didn't originally bring it up, but found the unemployed themselves talking about it, either with fear or resignation. For instance: I went to see a man aged twenty-eight. He had been out of steady work for six years. He lived on a houseboat and did odd jobs of salvaging and selling wood and iron. He told me that it took from three to six months for a man to stop going around looking for work. 'What's the use, you only wear out your only pair of shoes and then you get so disgusted.' That phrase, 'I get so disgusted . . .' is the one I most frequently hear to describe how they feel. You can understand what it means: it's a final admission of defeat or failure or both. Then the man began talking about the new works programme and he said, 'How many of them would work if they had the chance? How many of them even could work?'

Sometimes the unemployed themselves say: 'I don't know if I could do a real job right away, but I think I'd get used to it.'

The young are as disheartening as any group, more so, really. They are apathetic, sinking into a resigned bitterness. Their schooling, such as it is, is a joke; and they have never had the opportunity to learn a trade. They have no resources within or without; and they are waiting for nothing. They don't believe in man or God, let alone private industry; the only thing that keeps them from suicide is this amazing loss of vitality: they exist. 'I generally go to bed around seven at night, because that way you get the day over with quicker.'

NORMAN LEWIS
ESSEX

Essex is the ugliest county. I only went there to be able to work in peace and quiet and get away from the settlers from London south of the river. It was flat and untidy and full of water with the Colne and the Crouch and the Blackwater and all their tributaries fingering up from the sea and spreading vinous tendrils of water into the flat land. For half the year, the wind blew in from the east, over shingle, mud-flats, saltings and marshes: even twenty miles inland, where I first set up house, gulls drove the crows out of the fields.

In the late 1960s I found an empty farmhouse called Charmers End in the village of Long Crendon, took a three-year lease and settled in. Many of the farms and villages had odd, even poetic names—Crab's Green, Sweet Dew, Blythe Easter, Fantail and Honey Wood—although on the whole, the more fanciful the name the more dismal the place. When I moved in, there were black-and-white cows in a shining field at the bottom of the garden. The cows were responsible for my decision to take the place. Otherwise this part of Essex reminded me of the southern tip of South America, where the trees are deformed, a cold wind combs the grass and glum Indians, reserved and off-hand like the country people of Essex, are muffled in their clothes against the grey weather.

The farmer who had lived here had grown old alone and sold his land. One day he hauled himself to the top of the tallest tree in the garden, drank a quarter of a bottle of Lysol, shoved the barrel of a German pistol collected in the war into his mouth, and pulled the trigger. This man had also liked the cows. The new owner did not, and so they disappeared soon after.

The house was surrounded by a great moat, and all along its banks stood big white leafless trees which, stripped of their bark and dying, eventually fell into the water. It was like the Amazon. Some of the trees in the moat had lost their branches, and little remained but their trunks, turned grey and slimy like submerged alligators showing only the tips of their snouts above the surface. Those still standing provided an annual crop of an uncommon oyster fungus, collected by an Italian from Chelmsford. He called with a present of a bottle of Asti Spumante shortly after I moved in.

The Post Office found me a woman to clean up four days a week. She arrived on a horse, charging up the lane and across the moat, black hair streaming in the wind, another contribution to the Latin American aspect of this corner of Essex. With her fine, aquiline features and almond eyes she could easily have been an Indian of the plains under the eastern slope of the Andes, where the natives are tall and slender.

Dorothea was thirty-seven, handsome if not quite beautiful, with a partially disabled husband and a pretty daughter of twelve.

She immediately took control. She persuaded the pump to emit a dribble of water, removed the mummified jackdaw from the chimney, dropped a pebble to test the black and silken surface of the fluid in the septic tank, and nodded with satisfaction. She then went with me in the car to point out the bakers, the man who might agree to cut the grass and mow the lawn, and the one who could fix up a television aerial. We passed two men in baseball caps, chatting outside a pub. One wore dark glasses and a lumberjack shirt. 'Americans?' I asked.

'No, locals. Carpenters up at the base.'

'They look like Yanks.'

'Well, they want to, don't they? Most of the fellows work on the base these days. If you can call it work.'

Long Crendon was a long, narrow street straggling over the best part of a mile, hence its name. There was a bad smell at one end from a rubbish dump that looked like a collapsed volcano that had been smouldering for several years, and at the other from a pig farm. The houses were simple and plain, with white plastered fronts. The poorer and smaller ones were thatched, and some still had leaded lights. A substantial mansion standing in gardens back from the road had suffered brutal modernization, and the garden was now enclosed with a ranch-style fence. Until the previous month it had been named Hill Top, said Dorothea. Now, with a new owner who had been in property development, it had become Rancho Grande. It was the only evidence that money had been spent in the village, either on preservation or ornament.

We passed three depressing pubs and a grey little school with children squabbling in the playground. The church was the only building of note, with a Norman door, good stained glass and tombstones packed close in separate familial groups as if to carry earthly associations beyond the grave.

The tour ended with a passing glance at the village hall. 'That's where I go dancing with my friend Mr Short on Saturday night,' Dorothea said.

'Your friend?'

'Well, not my *boyfriend*. Actually I don't like him all that much. We just go dancing together. Otherwise I don't find him all that interesting. I expect you heard all about Dick's accident?'

'Doesn't Dick mind?'

Dorothea saw no reason why he should. 'He doesn't dance and he realizes I have to have some sort of break. Well, I mean it's only normal, isn't it?'

Later, I heard the gossip: that she was the target of village adulterers, who were encouraged by Dick, her complaisant husband.

I asked Dorothea why she had to ride. I mentioned that village opinion considered the horse a bad one, with the habit of tripping over its legs.

'It's an old jumper,' she said. 'It's not so much its legs as its back. It's hit the deck a few times.'

'They were telling me you were a member of one of the Cloate families, whatever they mean by that.'

'It's a sort of clan,' she said. 'The thing they have in Scotland. Dick and I belong to it. About half the village used to be Cloates, but there's only five families left now. They say only the Cloates were allowed to ride in the old days.'

'What else do you do besides ride horses?'

'Well, nothing really. We're supposed to help each other, but that's a laugh. Really, it's more a question of keeping in touch. You sometimes get Cloate people who've gone overseas writing home. I suppose they feel lonely out there. Maybe you write two or three letters and then it drops.'

'Nothing else?'

'We have a sort of get-together in August. There used to be about fifty of us, but now it's down to half that. A lot of these things are dying out.' She said times changed.

One interesting aspect of the Cloate personality was its attitude to education. For men, schooling was only a means to an end—usefulness and self-sufficiency—and the boys, having taken what the primary school had to offer, moved on as soon as possible to the education provided by life. In the old days, Dorothea had heard, a Cloate would always build his own house. The function of a girl, however, was to please. If she was plain and dull, there was nothing to be done, but if she showed promise—in beauty, even wit—no sacrifice was too great to develop her potential. Then she would be packed off to a boarding school—of an unassuming, yet rather special kind—in Woodford, London E11, where a village girl would be subjected to a process of transformation so great that at its end she was hardly recognizable, even to her own family.

First impressions often mislead. My original view of Long Crendon was of a poverty-stricken, backward Essex village, of the kind often described as 'unspoilt' because there was no money for necessary improvements. While every roof, thatched or otherwise, carried a television aerial, only a quarter of the houses had bathrooms, or even inside lavatories, and less than half were connected to the mains water supply or the sewer. Two buildings, the Rancho Grande and a pub, the Pied Bull, had central heating; otherwise coal fires burned, as ever, in small grates. The locals pretended contempt for luxuries city-dwellers everywhere took for granted, and there were villagers who boasted of leaving their windows open through the interminable Essex winter. That Long Crendon remained on the surface unchanged was a matter of stubborn conservatism and resistance to change rather than economics. Yet a hidden transformation was in progress. In 1943 the Americans had built an important base at Effingham, some five miles away, and since then, despite all local claims to a preference for the hard but worthy life, self-indulgence and luxury were making a stealthy appearance.

The Americans offered to employ every civilian capable of holding down a job. They paid well and were considerate, almost over-tolerant employers. Dorothea's Dick was one of the many who benefited. He had been considered unemployable after his accident, but as soon as he was able to get about he was taken on at the base as a timekeeper, an occupation for which nimbleness was not required. For some time Dorothea had kept him out of sight, but one day she brought him to see me. He was prematurely wizened and sat askew on a pony he controlled with one arm. The story was that while he was working twelve years before in an agricultural smithy, the prototype of a new combine harvester had run amok, snatched him up, neutered him, torn off a forearm, an ear and most of one foot. He and Dorothea had been married a matter of weeks when the accident occurred, and their daughter, Jane, had been conceived just in time.

I got to like Dick. According to the villagers, working for the Americans was like being on paid holiday. The main problem was finding a place to sleep undisturbed, because of the noise of the planes. Dick put his endless leisure to good use. He liked people, and limped about the place getting to know everybody and picking up useful gossip. He was a treasure house of village information, a holder of strong opinions and interested in religion.

'But you don't go to church, Dick?'

'Well, no. Most people round these parts don't.'

'And yet you're a believer?'

He gave a sly grin. 'When it suits me, I am. In the resurrection of the body, for instance. Now that's something I believe in. And I've every right to. It gives anybody like me a second chance, doesn't it? If the Bible says God can put back my missing bits, who am I to argue about it?' This, I supposed, was meant to be a joke.

In my second year at Long Crendon the new farmer moved in. The black-and-white cows had long gone, and the farmer now ploughed up the field and planted horse-beans, the most hideous of crops. My neighbour was thorough. The trees across the moat were on his land, and they all came down, whether dead or alive, and were cut up. He rode round on a tractor painted in astonishing psychedelic colours, like Sennacherib in his chariot, dealing death and destruction to nature. One of the big chemical firms was encouraging farmers to experiment with its sprays. He sprayed the banks of the moat and killed off a vast colony of frogs. The resident mallards, feeding on the frogs, also died. I watched them seized by a kind of paralysis, trying to take off. After splashing about in desperate fashion for a while they subsided and swam in slow tightening circles. In the end they could no longer hold their heads up, and finally drowned. In a single year this man changed everything in my Essex landscape. What looked in summer like the southern, treeless edge of the Argentine *pampas* became Siberia in winter. Nothing held back the east wind as it blew in from the North Sea. Six inches of snow lay in the ploughed fields. The wind plucked up the snow like feathers from a moulting goose and dropped it in the hollows of the land. When spring came there were still yard-deep pockets of frozen snow lying between the bare banks at the bottom of the lanes.

Every penny Dorothea and Dick scraped together was saved to send Jane to Woodford, but Jane was already thirteen and they were becoming desperate. Dorothea worked three days a week at the Rancho Grande, now owned by a man who had made a fortune from laundromats. Her beloved horse was for sale but there were no takers. She got permission to build on her garden and sold most of it to a speculator. This was a sacrifice indeed: endlessly enriched with the night soil from their cesspit, the garden produced vegetables of spectacular size and quality. Henceforth, she said, they would live on Cornish pasties with the occasional addition of sugar-beet leaves. These, which the farmers threw away, looked and tasted like spinach of an inferior kind. 'Are you really sure,' I asked, 'that what you're doing is for the best?'

But Dorothea insisted that Jane be given a proper start. She mentioned her cousins the Broadbents, accepted as the leading Cloate family. Bill and Emily Broadbent's daughter Patricia had just finished four years at Woodford, had gone straight from it to one of the leading schools for models and faced the prospect of a dazzling future. Pictures of her had begun to appear in the Essex newspapers, and there was talk of contracts. I made no attempt to dampen Dorothea's enthusiasm. But it was hard to believe that Jane—slouching about the village with rounded shoulders, pretty but vapid, burdened with a nasal and moaning Essex accent—could ever hope to imitate her cousin.

A few days later Dorothea cut several inches from Jane's lifeless hair, tidied up her finger-nails and took her to Woodford for an interview with Mrs Amos, headmistress of Gladben's Hall.

Mrs Amos was formidable, smooth-skinned, immaculate and precise. She unnerved Dorothea by the combination of her penetrating stare and an almost excessively sympathetic manner. There was something spiderish about her. 'But there you are,' Dorothea said. 'She gets the results.'

Jane, however, had been at her worst: fidgeting, embarrassed and tongue-tied. 'She couldn't have been more stupid,' Dorothea said.

'I want to know all about you,' Mrs Amos had said. 'Are you a sporty girl? Does music appeal to you, or do you like to curl up with a book?'

But Jane just sat there, Dorothea explained. 'She wouldn't utter. She wouldn't even look Mrs Amos in the face. There was a picture on the wall of a German battleship going down after some battle—was it the Battle of the Plate?—and she was hypnotized by it. "I'm sorry," I said to Mrs Amos. "It's just her nerves. It'll pass in a minute." I have to say Mrs Amos was very understanding. Full marks to her for that. She asked Jane what she wanted to do with her life and Jane told her she didn't know, and Mrs Amos said that was quite normal—most young people didn't. She was trying to draw Jane out,' Dorothea said, 'and so then she asked her what she did in the evening. Jane said she looked at the telly, but she didn't have any favourite programme: she just watched anything that happened to be on; it was all the same. Otherwise she went down to the bus shelter. That's what the kids do when there's nothing on the box. They just sit there.'

'So what was the outcome?' I asked.

'You won't believe this,' Dorothea said. 'She was accepted.'

'That's really tremendous news,' I said. 'You must be very happy and relieved.'

She was, and was worried now only about how she was going to come up with the money. But I was curious about what was taught at this school beside charm.

'Well,' Dorothea said, 'there's much more to it. I'll tell you exactly what Mrs Amos said to me. She said, "Here we introduce them to pride. Often when a girl first comes to us she has no ego, and therefore no personality, and we set out to change that. When she leaves us we expect her to be full of herself, and that in a woman is the Open Sesame to success.'"

With the coming of spring there were great changes in the neighbourhood. The Americans expanded the base, doubling their military personnel and building accommodation for families brought in on long-term postings. Once again, as it had been back in the forties, there were Americans everywhere. They were young, smartly uniformed and outstandingly polite, and local men who had sucked in humility with their mothers' milk were now amazed to be addressed as 'sir'.

The village began to smarten up. Essex had been discovered by the frontiersmen from London who paid dearly for arriving late on the scene. Charmers End, not worth £5,000 when I moved in, was expected to fetch at least five times that sum by the time my lease ran out. A half-dozen rather sombre-looking lath-and-plaster Jacobean buildings were snapped up. The newcomers stripped away plaster to expose ancient beams, knocked out partition walls to join up poky little rooms, put in cocktail bars and usually found a place somewhere for a wrought-iron Spanish ornamental gate. There was nothing to be done about a cesspit except lift the iron cover, peer in and drop it hastily back in place. The settlers from London cut down old diseased fruit trees to turn gardens into paddocks, and sometimes made the mistake of buying local horses on the cheap. They rose early to exercise fashionable dogs. For the first time the Pied Bull had vodka on sale, and the village shop now stocked yoghurt in various flavours.

A paternalistic US government assured military personnel volunteering for overseas service that the comforts awaiting them were no less complete than those they had come to expect at home, and so air transports began to fly in to Effingham laden with deep-freezers, washing-machines, pressure- and microwave cookers, hi-fi equipment, Hoovers, electric organs and even Persian carpets. Many of those for whom this flood of goods were destined had become accustomed to an annual trade-in, replacing old models with new, and a major disadvantage to the life overseas was that no regular outlets existed for discarded equipment. Thus, the efficient turnover of the entire system was threatened and a surplus built up, for the houses on base were small and soon glutted with gear.

Dick was everybody's friend. When consulted by the Americans about their quandary, he immediately discussed it with the local shopkeepers and affluent villagers such as the Broadbents; a number agreed to do what they could to ease the log-jam of consumer durables. It was the commitment to Jane's future that turned Dick into a salesman. First he accepted small gifts, then a trifling commission, then finally obliged American friends by giving them a price for some article for which there was no immediate sale and keeping it until a customer could be found. Thus trade developed. Dick was a reluctant and therefore good salesman, a little troubled about the legality of his enterprise, and there was a melancholic religiosity about him that reassured both seller and buyer.

Dorothea and Dick continued to live on Cornish pasties and sugar-beet tops. Dick did not like to talk about finance, but Dorothea told me that in the first few months of operations they added enough to the cache of money somewhere under the floor to pay for a year's schooling at Woodford. It was arranged that Jane would enter Gladben's in the coming September.

These mildly illicit activities brought Dick close to others of a more dangerous kind. He was approached by a senior sergeant newly arrived in the country with what sounded at first a tempting proposition. The sergeant had heard of Dick's connections and said that a source of supply of goods of a better kind had opened up. He showed Dick a Sears Roebuck catalogue and said that most of the items listed could be made available at about half price.

The feeling I had was that he had already half-committed himself, but something was clearly worrying him.

'The first thing you have to do is to find out where the stuff's coming from,' I told him.

'I have. It got sent here instead of to Germany and they're stuck with it up at the base.'

'Why don't they send it back?'

'He says there's no laid-down procedure. If it's here, it's here. They've got to get shot of it as best they can or it'll stay here forever.

All they want to do is recover the cost price.'

'Nobody will believe a story like that,' I told him. 'Where is it now?'

'In Warehouse 8. I've seen some of it.'

'How does this man strike you? Do you get the feeling he's a crook?'

'He's like any sergeant. A bit tough. They get used to ordering people about.'

I told Dick that I hoped he was not involved already, but that, if he was, he should get out of it as fast as he could. And so Dick went back and told the sergeant he wanted a day or two to think about it. The sergeant told him to keep his mouth shut.

A few days later Dick returned, full of excitement and alarm. He had been out fishing in a flooded gravel-pit at six in the morning when something happened that made him suspicious, and he asked me to come and see the place.

The site was where a company had been taking out gravel, pebbles and sand for as long as anybody could remember, and then suddenly had dropped everything and pulled out. This had happened ten or fifteen years before. In true Essex style there had been no attempt to tidy up before departure, and so now a half-dismantled pump protruded from the water and rails carried several shattered trucks down to the bullrushes sprouting on the verge of what was now a small lake. There were old breeze-blocks, oil barrels, a wheel-less vehicle sitting on its springs, and iron gates that opened wide upon further devastation. All these objects were host to the rank but vigorous creeping plants that would eventually muffle their outlines with coarse leaves and insignificant flowers.

Dick, very jumpy, insisted that we should pretend to fish, and we had taken rods with us. I fixed up my line and helped him to fix his. We then clambered down the bank and waded into the shallows among the bullrushes. A moorhen scuttled away dragging splashes across the water, and I breathed in the heavy odour of decaying vegetation and mud. It was a school holiday and two small boys were hacking with knives at the bushes and seedling trees. Part of a large brick and corrugated iron building showed among the elder trees on the far bank. It was reached, Dick said, by an overgrown track from the main road that he had seen a few days before. He had been down in the bushes by the water baiting his hook when a big US Air Force truck came down the track and stopped outside the building. Three US servicemen got out. Dick recognized one of them as the top sergeant. They unlocked the door of the building and began to unload packing cases from the truck and carry them in. It took them half-an-hour. Then they drove off.

'And what do you imagine it was all about?' I asked him.

'Stuff nicked from the base,' he said. 'I was shit-scared.'

'Why?'

'The sergeant. He'd have cut my throat if he saw me and thought I was spying on them.'

Dick explained how the racket worked. There was a fix back in the States with whoever handled the air schedules. Transports flying in always landed after the warehouses had been locked up for the night. The C-Van containers, unloaded and left in the parking bays—theoretically under armed guard—were promptly opened and up to a quarter of their contents spirited away. The consignment sheets corresponding to the abstracted goods were simply torn from the shipping documents and next morning the chief storeman cheerfully signed everything as OK.

'Why come to me about it?' I asked Dick.

'What do you think I ought to do?'

'Steer clear of it,' I said. I told him he should tell the sergeant anything he wanted and then keep away from him. I told him he should go somewhere else to fish.

Most of the married American servicemen and their families were content to stay on base, and the base did its best, with considerable success, to provide those things that made home sweet to them. England remained largely unknown. Only young servicemen ventured out, and when they did it was usually in search of female company. They were a godsend to the girls of Essex, which had become a sad backwater for young people. The Essex girls found the Americans more polite, considerate and enthusiastic than the English boys. In approaches to the opposite sex, the Americans often displayed an outmoded gallantry, which sometimes evoked pretended amusement but was always well received. Apart from drinking sessions in the pubs, Saturday night discos were about the only form of entertainment surviving in country places. A girl escorted to one by a local lad had to resign herself to a loutish rather than romantic experience. By contrast the weekend dances at the base offered a model of propriety and good order.

The calm, homely and rather formal atmosphere of the social club at the base seemed to exert a tranquillizing effect upon even the most unruly and pugnacious English males. Finding it impossible to pick a quarrel with their urbane American hosts, they soon gave up trying. Drinks at the base were better and much cheaper; the music was good and played on the very latest system; and the décor was tasteful and relaxing, and avoided cheap effects. No one was ever over-charged, and the old, sly trick practised in so many local clubs of turning up the heat to increase thirst and consumption was unnecessary, since American hospitality was not perverted by the profit-motive.

Above all, it was the servicemen themselves who impressed. The story had gone around that before arriving in Britain they had been issued with a booklet telling them how to behave. This struck all those who came into contact with them as absurd. These, the girls decided, were nature's gentlemen: handsome, clean-cut in both appearance and motive, sophisticated and rich. In the most discreet fashion, careful always not to provoke the rivalry of their English counterparts, the Americans showed photographs of themselves in their civilian days, often at the wheels of enormous cars, in the glamorous environment of their homeland: Santa Barbara and Beverly Hills, the Rocky Mountains, Yellowstone Park, Miami Beach and Disneyland. Few impressionable young girls could resist such an emotional assault. It was an experience that turned many a head. To Dorothea's horror, her daughter Jane was among them. Any girl under the age of seventeen, unless accompanied by her mother, was excluded from the magical Saturday night at the base. Jane—tall for her age—was dressed and made up by her friends to look at least eighteen and smuggled past the scrutiny at the door. She came home at midnight, defiant and smelling of alcohol; and Dorothea feared that, after this brief glimpse of paradise, Jane would never settle for the monotony of Long Crendon again. But it was July, and the dangerous weeks were coming to an end. 'Only a couple of months to go and she'll be safely out of harm's way at Woodford,' Dorothea said. 'My feeling is we're just in time.'

After our visit to the old gravel pit, Dick was under a cloud. He could not shake himself free from the attentions of the sinister sergeant, who refused to allow him to break what he claimed was an agreement, and began to adopt a threatening posture. Then suddenly the man dropped out of sight. The English detectives on permanent duty with the base police toured the village with his photograph, and took statements, including one from Dick, but there the matter was dropped. Dick learned that the sergeant had been arrested and packed off in handcuffs back to the States. The transports ceased to land after dark, and the volume of American luxury goods in circulation went into steep decline. Some time later, as a matter of curiosity, Dick visited the old shed where he had seen the crates unloaded and found it open and empty.

'It has all been a bit of a fright,' Dick said. Now, suddenly, he was nervous about his involvement in the disposal of the base families' surplus gear. Dick had learned that such imported items were for personal use only. Somebody had broken a law, but Dick was not sure whose law it was, and who had done the breaking. The visits of the detective occasioned further unease. The villagers interviewed would have been crafty enough to keep him out of the kitchens where any piece of machinery of American origin would certainly be on view. Still, one never knew. A man like that was trained to use his eyes. Despondently, Dick decided to play safe and pull out of the business, and then, just as his hopes for Jane's future began to recede, new prospects for commerce opened up.

The idea of status had hardly reached Long Crendon at the time of my arrival, and the alterations made by the newcomers to the houses they bought were seen by the natives as unreasoning and eccentric. Why, the villagers argued, should a man enclose his garden with a fence that kept nothing out? Why, instead of spending a hundred or two on renovating a barn, should he have it rebuilt in Norman style at a cost of £2,000?

Slowly an inkling of what was behind this madness began to seep in. Here and there a villager became infected with it. The problem was how, in their gentle and unassertive manner, could village people acquire the magical property that enabled a man to stand out from his fellows? Nothing a man could do to alter his house—by a lick of paint on the outside or a glass front door or a chiming bell—could conceal the stark facts, known to all, of pump-water and outside privy. Almost every employable male worked at the base for a similar salary: village life was one of total equality; all were at the bottom of the pyramid. Humility had been inherited from the feudal servility of a not too distant past. Now suddenly the idea was abroad that a man could be 'different'—command a little more than average respect. Nothing could be done about the house, but, as Dick pointed out, the possession of a good car, for example, could set a man apart, and by cutting down expenses, such a prize could come within reach.

American servicemen normally arrived in the country for a three-year tour of duty, and often brought their cars with them. When the time came to move on, they were quite ready to part with the vehicle at a reasonable price. Dick had discovered this and acted accordingly. He came to an agreement with the Customs over the matter of excise duty, and after some trial and error, was able to cope with the paperwork required. Everyone knew Dick and knew that they would get value for money. Within a few months many of Long Crendon's cottages had a shining American car parked outside.

After Christmas and Easter the third most important feast celebrated in Long Crendon was the ancient secular one of August Bank Holiday. At this the Cloates, for all their slow loss of power and influence, appeared together as a clan, and assisted by alcohol the old defiant spirit flickered strongly.

On the bank holiday the people of Long Crendon who normally preferred to stay inside when not working felt suddenly and briefly the mysterious call of the open, and gathered up their families to go to the sea-shore or on picnics amid the few trees that remained where there once had been woods. It was almost a point of honour to escape from confining walls. The local pubs which normally served, at best, a sandwich at the bar provided full-scale lunches. The traditional holiday dish was eel pie, although Long

Crendon was possibly the last place in Essex where it could be tasted. It was not what it had been, since the eels were no longer caught in the Blackwater or Crouch, but imported frozen from Holland. Nevertheless, eel pie was not to be avoided on this occasion.

Several tables had been reserved for the Cloates in the pleasant garden at the back of the Pied Bull. Some of the family had moved away from the area but made the effort to be present at the annual reunion. Of these family members I knew nothing at all. Nor had I had contacts with the Cloates living in the village who were notorious for keeping to themselves. I knew only Dorothea and Dick, and their cousins the Broadbents.

For both families this was an exceptional occasion. Both Jane and Patricia would soon be saying goodbye to the village for a while: Jane to face whatever Mrs Amos had in store for her; Patricia, having completed with distinction her course at the school for models, to join a party of them visiting Brazil, where they were to be photographed wearing the creations of a famous couturier against that pageant of water, the Iguazu Falls.

I drove Dick down to the Pied Bull and we had a drink in the bar while waiting for the others. Soon Dorothea came into sight with Emily and Bill Broadbent, all on horseback. Patricia broke with the custom. She was dropped off at the pub by the Cambridge-educated son of a local landowner who drove her in his Porsche.

Dick left me. I walked to the door of the bar to stand for a moment. A faint scent of eel pie was in my nostrils, and I looked down on this gathering of the clans. At this level success made itself felt, and Bill Broadbent, a once handsome saloon-bar joker, now prematurely aged by the good life his asset-stripping had provided, was surrounded by family toadies who had not done so well, a single gin and tonic held in every hand. These men were less prosperous than the average villager. Some were too old to be employed at the base, and some declined the opportunity, speaking of private means. Apart from Bill, only two had come on horseback. The Essex historian Stephen Maudsley, writing at the end of the last century, had mentioned the great-grandfathers of these men. 'Scant heed was paid to law and order in these remote parts. Scarcely a score of years have passed since the notorious Cloates of Crendon's

End raided a nearby village which had given them some offence.'
This seemed like the end of the road.

Jane and Patricia had moved out of the crowd and were
walking together. They were fond of each other. Patricia, described
by Mrs Amos as possibly her most finished product, floated,
drifted, seeming at times almost to be airborne, while Jane plodded
at her side as if carrying a sack of potatoes on her shoulders.
Patricia's svelte body was clad to perfection. By comparison Jane
appeared outlandish, almost tribal, as so many village girls were. In
defiance of Dorothea's protests, she had applied bleach to her hair,
followed by a bizarre attack with scissors. Patricia was pleasant and
gracious, fluttering the tips of her fingers at anyone greeting her
who could not easily be reached. Jane ignored these gestures. Both
girls were smiling, and studying them as they came close I
understood that Patricia's smile was part of Mrs Amos's art—an
asset, an accomplishment which matched the other ingredients of
her beauty. Jane's smile, for all her lumpishness, was human—
fallible, but sweet.

Soon after, a project took me to the Far East, off and on for
nearly four years. I felt involved in Long Crendon and its
problems, and before leaving I tried to secure a base there by
buying Charmers Green, but the asking price was beyond my
means. Nevertheless I kept in touch with Dorothea. We exchanged
letters two or three times a year. Things continued to go fairly well
for them. Her first letter informed me that she had sold her horse,
and that she and Dick now owned a veteran but serviceable MG.
After that, their gracious but shattered house, with the remnant of
its incomparable vegetable patch and its cracked rear wall, went to
a buyer from London and they moved into a brand-new bungalow.
The view was of other bungalows.

Dick had been treated, and was now able to stand up straight
and had taken a course in public speaking. But most of her news
concerned Jane. 'It's just as they told us it would be,' she said. 'The
year's not up yet and you can hardly believe the difference. It's
wonderful what they can do.'

By the next year Jane's speech had been dealt with to
everybody's satisfaction. 'You remember the way she used to

mumble? I could hardly understand what she was saying myself. Now she speaks as clear as anybody. But she doesn't sound too la-di-da with it if you know what I mean. Which is rather nice.'

Letters in the third year indicated that Jane might have started to think for herself. 'She's been awarded a prize for social awareness, whatever they mean by that,' Dorothea wrote. 'I suppose we're the tiniest bit disappointed because modelling's out. She says it's not for her. Mrs Amos says she's clever enough to do anything she wants, but we shouldn't attempt to sway her. While we're on the subject, did you hear about Patricia? She's always in the papers these days. Do you remember when she was just off to Brazil? Well, she married a Brazilian landowner with an estate the size of Essex. The paper said he was the seventh richest man in the world.' The latest story was that the marriage was on the rocks. Money wasn't everything, Dorothea noted.

By the time of her last letter, Dorothea's disappointment with her daughter seemed to have deepened. 'Mind you,' she wrote, 'whatever we've done for her, we'd do it all over again. Her father and I have written to suggest that she might consider being something like a personal secretary to an MP, or a television presenter. She says we'll talk about it when she comes home for the holidays. She hasn't had much to say about herself, which doesn't seem a good sign. The news of Patricia isn't so good. I sent you a cutting about her divorce from the Brazilian. Now she's married a French count with a castle in Angoulême. He's more than twice her age. Sometimes I wonder. Her mother can't see this one lasting long either. I always say happiness is what counts.'

I found myself once more in Long Crendon. The changes, although more radical than expected, had not been unforeseen. It was remarkable that so dramatic a face-lift could have been achieved in so short a time. The villagers had done whatever they could to make the place ugly within their resources, adding a little raw red brick here, an atrocious plastic ornament there, but it was the newcomers who had set to work to strip every vestige of character. There were many newcomers now. In their total isolation they formed an ethnic minority. They searched for the picturesque and were able to finance change from limitless funds.

Certain iniquities had been suppressed. The smouldering refuse dump had been removed and the health authorities had curbed the smellier operations at the pig farm. Main drainage had come to the long street at last, thus—except in the case of outlying houses—putting an end to the collection of night soil which had produced so many superb vegetables in the past. All three austere old pubs had been tarted up. I stayed at the Pied Bull. Its simple façade was tricked out with coloured lights and a sign of Pre-Raphaelite inspiration had been hung, showing a bull without testicles. In the past, narrow, straight-backed wall benches had enforced dignity upon the patrons. Now they lounged in armchairs upholstered in buttoned pink plastic. At Charmers End the moat had been sanitized and given a concrete landing stage, to which a black gondola with a lamp on its prow was tied. The house had statuary and a double garage, and it could only be glimpsed through the sombre foliage of the *Cupressus leylandii*, now to be seen everywhere in Long Crendon.

My conviction that the village was destined to become a cultural colony of the United States had proved well founded, but the process had been swifter than I would have thought possible. Two cars were parked outside many of the village houses, some of them fish-tailed monsters. Matters of fundamental custom, such as mealtimes, had been revolutionized. For centuries, country people everywhere had sat down at twelve-thirty prompt to stuff themselves with the main meal of the day, and had then risen from the table to burn off the stodgy food by hard physical work in the field.

Such work was now a thing of the past, and gone with it was the traditional midday meal. Men employed at the base no longer wished to consume a pound and a half of potatoes every lunchtime, and had fallen in with the American system of a quick and easily digested meal, followed by something more substantial in the evening. Chilli con carne was the current favourite. A few of the more advanced families joined with American friends to celebrate Thanksgiving: butterball turkey and all the trimmings flown in from the US. The local English, apart from the newcomers, were becoming less reclusive. Even in the recent past they had lived their private, separate lives behind tightly drawn curtains. Now they organized get-togethers in the American fashion. Pabst and Schlitz beer were drunk from cans. Pre-cooked, containerized foods from Indian and Chinese take-aways were served on cardboard plates and eaten with plastic cutlery. These accessories were smuggled out with little difficulty from the base. The memory in Long Crendon of poverty once endured was fading fast.

Dorothea and Dick were in their bungalow. They were no longer under a strain. A bungalow—with furniture polished and in place, the comforting sound of the toilet's flush and no major cracks in the wall—can act as a tranquillizer. Dick's nervous tic, which had once surfaced every few minutes in the wrinkles round his mouth, was gone, and the doctors, in straightening him out, had added an inch to his height. Dorothea had put on a few pounds and was all the better for it, and a hairdresser had brought life to the lank black Indian hair of old.

Dick was as busy as ever. Within minutes of my arrival he was summoned by telephone. He was running a little agency affair of his own, Dorothea said. Accommodation was very short in a rapidly expanding area, and he was doing what he could to help out. He had at last found the Lord. Many of his friends from the States were Baptists, and he had become one as well. Dorothea put in a few hours most days, as ever, at Charmers End, not because they needed the money with Jane now more or less off their hands, but because she liked having something to do.

Jane had been home for three months. 'Isn't that earlier than intended?' I asked.

'We had a long talk with Mrs Amos,' she said, 'after which there didn't seem much point in going any further.'

'In what direction? You told me Jane had decided against modelling. What about the other possibilities? It sounded as though Mrs Amos had high hopes for her.'

'According to Mrs Amos, Jane was exceptionally gifted. She was attractive and intelligent, and she could have done anything she wanted to.' Dorothea gestured resignation.

'But she didn't want to be a television presenter or anybody's personal secretary?'

'It was her whole attitude. That kind of thing didn't seem to mean anything to her. In one way, Mrs Amos said, she'd turned out better than hoped, and in another year she could have had the world at her feet. But it all left her cold.'

I told Dorothea that I was beginning to suspect she was to be congratulated. She had an interesting daughter.

'Mrs Amos said you sometimes come across people you thought you could change, and they fooled you by pretending to go along, but really underneath they were going their own way all the time.'

So Jane had beaten the system, I said; she had survived.

'I suppose that's one way of looking at it,' Dorothea said. 'Anyway, we brought her home.'

I asked what she was going to do.

'She's filling in time in the accounts office at the base.'

'And after that?'

'She'll take up nursing.'

'What could be better?'

'You won't be surprised to hear she has an American boyfriend.'

'Why should I be surprised? What is he—a pilot, or a navigator?'

'No,' she said. 'He's on the catering side. An assistant cook.'

I was struck by inspiration and asked: 'Would he by any chance be coloured?'

'How on earth did you guess?'

It was just something that had occurred to me. I said, 'We're getting to know Jane. Both of us. What time do you expect her home? I'm much looking forward to seeing her.'

SEAMUS DEANE
FEET

The plastic table-cloth hung so far down that I could see only their feet. But I could hear the noise and some of the talk, although I was so crunched up inside that I could make out very little of what they were saying. Besides, Smoky was whimpering as he cuddled up on my stomach and I could feel his body quivering every so often under his fur; every quiver made me deaf to their words and alert to their noise.

He had found me under the table when the room filled with feet, standing at all angles, and he sloped through them and came to huddle himself on me. He felt the dread too. She was going to die after they took her to the hospital. I could hear the clumping of the feet of the ambulance men as they tried to manoeuvre her on a stretcher down the stairs. They would have to lift it high over the banister; the turn was too narrow. The stretcher had red handles. I had seen them when the shiny shoes of the ambulance men appeared in the centre of the room. One had been holding it, folded up, perpendicular, with the handles on the ground beside his shiny black shoes which had a tiny redness in one toe-cap when he put the stretcher handles on to the linoleum. The lino itself was so shiny that there was a redness in it too, at an angle, buried in it like a warmth just under the surface. Una was so hot this morning that, pale and sweaty as she was, she made me think of redness too. It came off her, like heat from a griddle. Her eyes shone with pain and pressure, inflated from the inside.

This was a new illness. I loved the names of the others— diphtheria, scarlet fever or scarletina, rubella, polio, influenza; they almost always ended in an 'o' or an 'a' and made me think of Italian football-players or racing drivers or chess-players. Besides, each had its own smell, especially diphtheria, because of the disinfected sheets that were hung over the bedroom doors and billowed out their acrid fragrances in the draughts that chilled your ankles on the stairs. Even the mumps, which came after the diphtheria, was a sickness that did not frighten, because the word was as funny as the shape of everybody's face, all swollen, as if there had been a terrific fight. But this was a new sickness. This was called meningitis. It was a word you had to bite on to say it. It had a fright and a hiss in it. It didn't make me think of anything except Una's eyes widening all the time and getting lighter, as if helium were

pumping into them from her brain. They would burst, I thought, unless they could find a way of getting all that pure helium pain out. I wondered if they could.

They were at the bottom of the stairs. All the feet moved that way. I could see Uncle Manus's brown shoes; the heels were worn down, and he was hesitating, moving back and forward a little. Uncle Dan and Uncle Tom had identical shoes, heavy and rimed with mud and cement, because they had come from the building site in Creggan. Dan's were dirtier, though, because Tom was the foreman. But they weren't good shoes. Dan put one knee up on a chair and I squirmed flat to see the scabs on the sole of the one that was in mid-air. There was putlock oil on his socks and black bars of it on the sole. But it was my mother's and father's feet that I watched most. She was wearing low heels that badly needed mending, and her feet were always swollen so that, even from there, I could see the shoe leather embedded, vanishing into her ankles.

There was more scuffle and noise and her feet disappeared into the hallway, after the stretcher, and she was cough-crying as my father's work-boots followed close behind her, huge, with the laces thonged round the back. Then everybody went out and the room was empty.

Smoky shook under his fur. It was cold in there with all the doors open and the winter air darkening. She was going to die and she was younger than me. She was only six. I tried to imagine her not there. She would go to heaven, for sure. Wouldn't she miss us? What could you do in heaven, except smile? All the same, she had a great smile.

Everybody came in again. There wasn't much talking. My father stood near the table. I could smell the quays off his dungarees, the aroma of horizons where ships grew to a speck and disappeared. Every day he went to work I felt he was going out foreign, as we said; and every day when he came back, I was relieved that he had changed his mind. Tom was pushing a spirit-level into a long leg-pocket of his American boiler suit, and Dan picked up his coat, which had fallen off a chair on to the floor. I could see the dermatitis stains on his fingers and knuckles. He was allergic to the plaster he had to work with every day. Next month, he'd be off work, his hands all scabs and sores. Where would Una be next month?

They all left except my parents. He was at the table again, very close. My mother was standing at the press-cupboard, a couple of feet away, her shoes pressed together, looking very small. She was still crying. My father's boots moved towards her until they were very close. He was saying something. Then he got closer, almost stood on her shoes, which moved apart. One of his boots was between her feet. There was her shoe, then his boot, then her shoe, then his boot. I looked at Smoky, who licked my face. He was kissing her. She was still crying. Their feet shifted and I thought she was going to fall for one shoe came off the ground for a second. Then they steadied and they just stood there like that and everything was silent and I scarcely breathed.

That was my first death. When the priest tossed the first three shovelfuls of clay on to the coffin, the clattering sound seemed to ring all over the hillside graveyard and my father's face moved sideways as if he had been struck.

We were all lined up on the lip of the grave which was brown and narrow, so much so that the ropes they had looped through the coffin handles came up stained with the dun earth. One of the gravediggers draped the ropes over a headstone before he started heaving the great mound of clay on top of her. The clay came up to the brim as though it were going to boil over. We placed flowers and leaned our hands on the cold earth as we had leaned them on the glossy coffin top and as we had pressed them on her waxen hands the night before at the wake, where one candle burned and no drink was taken. When we got back, the candle was out and my mother was being comforted by aunts and neighbours who all wore the same serious and determined expression of compassion and sternness, so that even the handsome and the less-than-handsome all looked alike. The men doffed their caps and looked into the distance. No one looked anyone else in the face, it seemed.

The children appeared here and there, their faces at angles behind or between adults, fascinated, like angels staring into the light. I went up to the bedroom where she had lain and sat on my bed and looked at hers and buried my face in the pillow where her pain had been, saying her name inside my head but not out loud, breathing for something of her but only finding the scent of cotton, soap, of a life rinsed out and gone. When I heard noise on the stairs, I came out to see my uncles lifting the third bed from that downstairs room up over the banisters. They told me to stand aside as they worked it into the room and put the bed where she was waked beside the bed where she had been sick. The wake bed was a better one, with a headboard. Deirdre or Eilis would have a bed to herself.

Una came back only once, some weeks later. My mother had asked me to visit the grave and put flowers on it. They would have to be wild flowers, since shop flowers were too expensive. I forgot until it was almost four o'clock and getting dark. I ran to the graveyard, hoping it would not be shut. But it was too late. The gates were padlocked. I cut up the lane alongside the east wall until I reached the corner where the wall had collapsed about two feet from the top. It was easy to climb over and inside there was an untended area where the grass was long and where I had seen flowers growing before. But there were none, not even on the stunted hedgerow beneath the wall—not a berry, not a husk. I pulled some long grass and tried to plait it, but it was too wet and slippery. I threw the long stems away into the mottled air and they fell apart as they disappeared.

Running between the little pathways which separated the graves, I got lost several times before I found the fresh grave and recognized the withered flowers as those we had left a short time before. I pulled the wreaths apart, hoping to find some flowers not so badly withered, but there were very few. A torn rose, a chrysanthemum as tightly closed as a nut, some irises that were merely damp stalks with a tinge of blue—that was all. But I couldn't get them to hold together with the bits of wire from the original wreaths, so I scooped at the ground and put them in a bunch together, pressing the earth round them with my foot. All the while, I was saying her name over and over. Una, Una, Una, Una, Una. It was dark and I felt contrite and lonely, fearful as well. 'I have to go,' I said to the ground, 'I have to go. I don't like leaving you, but

I have to go, Una.' The wall seemed far away. I got up off my knees and rubbed my hands on my socks. 'I'll come back soon. 'Bye.'

I set off at a run, along the dark pathways, zig-zagging round headstones and great glass bells in which flowers were stifling, Celtic crosses, raised statues, lonely, bare plots, a fresh grave where the flowers still had some colour even in the light that the trees were swallowing into their trunks and branches. She came right down the path before me for an instant, dressed in her usual tartan skirt and jumper, her hair tied in ribbons, her smile sweeter than ever. Even as I said her name she wasn't there and I was running on, saying her name again, frightened now, until I reached the wall and looked back from the broken top stones over the gloomy hillside and its heavy burden of dead. Then I ran again until I reached the street-lamps on the Lone Moor Road, and scraped the mud off my shoes against the kerb and brushed what I could of it from my clothes. I walked home, slowly. I was late but being a bit later did not matter now. I didn't know if I would tell or not; that depended on what I was asked. I knew it would upset my mother, but, then again, it might console her to think Una was still about, although I wished she wasn't wandering about that graveyard on her own.

My older brother, Liam, settled the issue for me. I met him in the street and told him instantly. At first he was amused, but then got angry when I wondered aloud if I should tell my mother. 'Are you out of your head, or what? You'd drive her mad; she's out of her mind anyway sending you for flowers this time o' year. Sure any half-sane person would have said Yes and done nothing. Anyway, you saw nothing. You say nothing. You're not safe to leave alone.'

All night I lay thinking of her and hearing again the long wail of agony from my mother half-way through the family rosary. It made everybody stand up and Smoky crawled back under the table. I wished I could go in there with him but we all just stood there as she cried and pulled her hair and almost fought my father's consoling arms away. All her features were so stretched I hardly recognized her. It was like standing in the wind at night, listening to her. She cried all night. Every so often I would hear her wail, so desolate it seemed distant, and I thought of Una in the graveyard, standing under all those towering stone crosses, her ribbons red.

JEANETTE
WINTERSON
ORION

H ere are the co-ordinates: five hours, thirty minutes right ascension (the co-ordinate on the celestial sphere analogous to longitude on earth) and zero declination (at the celestial equator). Any astronomer can tell where you are.

It's different isn't it from head back in the garden on a frosty night sensing other worlds through a pair of binoculars? I like those nights. Kitchen light out and wearing Wellingtons with shiny silver insoles. On the wrapper there's an astronaut showing off his shiny silver suit. A short trip to the moon has brought some comfort back to earth. We can wear what Neil Armstrong wore and never feel the cold. This must be good news for star-gazers whose feet are firmly on the ground. We have moved with the times. And so will Orion.

Every 200,000 years or so, the individual stars within each constellation shift position. That is, they are shifting all the time, but more subtly than any tracker dog of ours can follow. One day, if the earth has not voluntarily opted out of the solar system, we will wake up to a new heaven whose dome will again confound us. It will still be home but not a place to take for granted. I wouldn't be able to tell you the story of Orion and say, 'Look, there he is, and there's his dog Sirius whose loyalty has left him bright.' The dot-to-dot log-book of who we were is not a fixed text. For Orion, who was the result of three of the gods in a good mood pissing on an ox-hide, the only tense he recognized was the future continuous. He was a mighty hunter. His arrow was always in flight, his prey endlessly just ahead of him. The carcasses he left behind became part of his past faster than they could decay. When he went to Crete he didn't do any sunbathing. He rid the island of all its wild beasts. He could really swing a cudgel.

Stories abound. Orion was so tall that he could walk along the sea bed without wetting his hair. So strong he could part a mountain. He wasn't the kind of man who settles down. And then he met Artemis, who wasn't the kind of woman who settles down either. They were both hunters and both gods. Their meeting is recorded in the heavens, but you can't see it every night, only on certain nights of the year. The rest of the time Orion does his best to dominate the skyline, as he always did.

Our story is the old clash between history and home. Or to put it another way, the immeasurable impossible space that seems to divide the hearth from the quest.

Listen to this.

On a wild night, driven more by weariness than by common sense, King Zeus decided to let his daughter do it differently: she didn't want to get married and sit out some war while her man, god or not, underwent the ritual metamorphosis from palace prince to craggy hero; she didn't want children. She wanted to hunt. Hunting did her good.

By morning she had packed and set off for a new life in the woods. Soon her fame spread and other women joined her but Artemis didn't care for company. She wanted to be alone. In her solitude she discovered something very odd. She had envied men their long-legged freedom to roam the world and return full of glory to wives who only waited. She knew about the history-makers and the home-makers, the great division that made life possible. Without rejecting it, she had simply hoped to take on the freedoms that belonged to the other side. What if she travelled the world and the seven seas like a hero? Would she find something different or the old things in different disguises? She found that the whole world could be contained within one place because that place was herself. Nothing had prepared her for this.

The alchemists have a saying, *Tertium non data*. The third is not given. That is, the transformation from one element into another, from waste matter into best gold is a process that cannot be documented. It is fully mysterious. No one really knows what effects the change. And so it is with the mind that moves from its prison to a vast plain without any movement at all. We can only guess at what happened.

One evening when Artemis had lost her quarry, she lit a fire where she was and tried to rest. But the night was shadowy and full of games. She saw herself by the fire: as a child, a woman, a hunter, a Queen. Grabbing the child, she lost sight of the woman and when she drew her bow the Queen fled. What would it matter if she crossed the world and hunted down every living creature as long as her separate selves eluded her? In the end when no one was left, she would have to confront herself. Leaving home meant leaving nothing behind. It came too, all of it, and waited in the dark. She realized that the only war worth fighting was the one that raged within; the rest were all diversions. In this small space, her hunting miles, she was going to bring herself home. Home was not a place for the faint-hearted; only the very brave could live with themselves.

In the morning she set out, and set out every morning day after day.

In her restlessness she found peace.

Then Orion came.

He wandered into Artemis's camp, scattering her dogs and bellowing like a bad actor, his right eye patched and his left arm in a splint. She was a mile or so away fetching water. When she returned she saw this huge rag of a man eating her goat. Raw. When he'd finished with a great belch and the fat still fresh around his mouth, he suggested they take a short stroll by the sea's edge. Artemis didn't want to but she was frightened. His reputation hung around him like bad breath. The ragged shore, rock-pitted and dark with weed, reminded him of his adventures and he unravelled them in detail while the tide came in up to her waist. There was nowhere he hadn't been, nothing he hadn't seen. He was faster than a hare and stronger than a pair of bulls. He was as good as a god.

'You smell,' said Artemis, but he didn't hear.

Eventually he allowed her to wade in from the rising water and light a fire for them both. No, he didn't want her to talk; he knew about her already. He'd been looking for her. She was a curiosity; he was famous. What a marriage.

But Artemis did talk. She talked about the land she loved and its daily changes. This was where she wanted to stay until she was ready to go. The journey itself was not enough. She spoke quickly, her words hanging on to each other; she'd never told anyone before. As she said it, she knew it was true, and it gave her strength to get up and say goodbye. She turned. Orion raped Artemis and fell asleep.

She thought about that time for years. It took a few moments only and she was really aware of only the hair of his stomach that was matted with sand, scratching her skin. When he'd finished, she pushed him off already snoring. His snores shook the

134

earth. Later, in the future, the time would remain vivid and unchanged. She wouldn't think of it differently; she wouldn't make it softer or harder. She would just keep it and turn it over in her hands. Her revenge had been swift, simple and devastatingly ignominious. She killed him with a scorpion.

In a night, 200,000 years can pass, time moving only in our minds. The steady marking of the seasons, the land well-loved and always changing, continues outside, while inside, light years move us on to landscapes that revolve under different skies.

Artemis lying beside dead Orion sees her past changed by a single act. The future is still intact, still unredeemed, but the past is irredeemable. She is not who she thought she was. Every action and decision has led her here. The moment has been waiting the way the top step of the stairs waits for the sleep-walker. She had fallen and now she is awake. As she looks at the sky, the sky is peaceful and exciting. A black cloak pinned with silver brooches that never need polish. Somebody lives there for sure, wrapped up in the glittering folds. Somebody who recognized that the journey by itself is never enough and gave up spaceships long ago in favour of home.

On the beach the waves made pools of darkness around Artemis's feet. She kept the fire burning, warming herself and feeling Orion grow slowly cold. It takes some time for the body to stop playing house.

The fiery circle that surrounded her contained all the clues she needed to recognize that life is for a moment in one shape then released into another. Monuments and cities would fade away like the people who built them. No resting-place or palace could survive the light years that lay ahead. There was no history that would not be rewritten, and the earliest days were already too far away to see. What would history make of tonight?

Tonight is clear and bright with a cold wind stirring the waves into peaks. The foam leaves slug trails in rough triangles on the sand. The salt smell bristles the hair inside her nostrils; her lips are dry. She's thinking about her dogs. They feel like home because she feels like home. The stars show her how to hang in space supported by nothing at all. Without medals or certificates or territories she owns, she can burn as they do, travelling through time until time stops and eternity changes things again. She has noticed that change doesn't hurt her.

It's almost light, which means the disappearing act will soon begin. She wants to lie awake watching until the night fades and the stars fade and the first grey-blue slates the sky. She wants to see the sun slash the water. But she can't stay awake for everything; some things have to pass her by. So what she doesn't see are the lizards coming out for food or Orion's eyes turned glassy overnight. A small bird perches on his shoulder, trying to steal a piece of his famous hair.

Artemis waited until the sun was up before she trampled out the fire. She brought rocks and stones to cover Orion's body from the eagles. She made a high mound that broke the thudding wind as it scored the shore. It was a stormy day, black clouds and a thick orange shining on the horizon. By the time she had finished, she was soaked with rain. Her hands were bleeding, her hair kept catching in her mouth. She was hungry but not angry now.

The sand that had been blonde yesterday was now brown with wet. As far as she could see there was the grey water white-edged and the birds of prey wheeling above it. Lonely cries and she was lonely, not for friends but for a time that hadn't been violated. The sea was hypnotic. Not the wind or the cold could move her from where she sat like one who waited. She was not waiting; she was remembering. She was trying to find what it was that had brought her here. The third is not given. All she knew was that she had arrived at the frontiers of common sense and crossed over. She was safe now. No safety without risk, and what you risk reveals what you value.

She stood up and in the getting-dark walked away, not looking behind her but conscious of her feet shaping themselves in the sand. Finally, at the headland, after a bitter climb to where the woods bordered the steep edge, she turned and stared out, seeing the shape of Orion's mound, just visible now, and her own footsteps walking away. Then it was fully night, and she could see nothing to remind her of the night before except the stars.

And what of Orion? Dead but not forgotten. For a while he was forced to pass the time in Hades, where he beat up flimsy beasts and cried a lot. Then the gods took pity on him and drew him up to themselves and placed him in the heavens for all to see. When he rises at dawn, summer is nearly here. When he rises in the evening, beware of winter and storms. If you see him at midnight, it's time to pick the grapes. He has his dogs with him, Canis Major and Canis Minor and Sirius, the brightest star in our galaxy. Under his feet, if you care to look, you can see a tiny group of stars: Lepus, the hare, his favourite food.

Orion isn't always at home. Dazzling as he is, like some fighter pilot riding the sky, he glows very faint, if at all, in November. November being the month of Scorpio.

NUMBERS

This photograph shows Fernando Pessoa, who was born in Portugal one hundred years ago.

He is regarded as Portugal's greatest 20th Century poet.

He wrote much but published little in his lifetime.

He was one of the most inventive geniuses of the modern movement.

His radical solution to the problem of identity was to split himself into four people: Alberto Caeiro, Ricardo Reis, Álvaro de Campos – and Fernando Pessoa. Each was a distinctive poet with his own style, subject matter and biography.

NUMBERS

NUMBERS is Britain's newest and best poetry magazine.

NUMBERS 4, appearing this June, will contain a celebration of Pessoa's centenary. This will include:

- translations of his Portuguese poems
- poems he wrote in English
- extracts from his fiction
- a biographical introduction
- a critical essay by Octavio Paz

NUMBERS 4 will also contain a wide variety of new English poetry and prose.

Here are four of the most important poets of the 20th century. They are all in the latest issue of NUMBERS.

———— ★ ————

JONATHAN MILLER
AMONG CHICKENS

1

I never had a sense of humour. What started me in a theatrical direction was finding at a very early age that I had a talent. In fact, not so much a talent as a disability: I could impersonate chickens. I *was* a chicken. I said to people, 'I will imitate a chicken for you,' and this pleased them. I don't know why. It did. Therefore I became extremely observant of the minute dialect of chickens.

For example, I became very interested in this double thing they have: it starts off with '*buk, buk, buk, buk*', and then '*bacagh*' follows. I noticed that some of the cruder impersonators of chickens, and there were competitors at school, never understood that there was a rather subtle variation of '*buk, buk, buk*' for every '*bacagh*'. They used to think it was absolutely regular. But I noticed, and this was really a big breakthrough in chicken linguistics, that chickens liked to lead you up the garden path. They would lead you to expect that for every four or five '*buk*' there would be a '*bacagh*'; so people, the bad chicken impersonators, the unobservant ones, would go as follows: '*Buk, buk, buk, buk, bacagh, buk, buk, buk, buk, bacagh, buk, buk, buk, buk, buk, bacagh.*' What I noticed, after prolonged examination, was an entirely different pattern of chicken speech behaviour. Thus: '*Buk, buk, buk, buk, buk, buk, bacagh, buk, buk, bacagh, buk, buk, buk, buk, buk, buk, buk, buk, buk . . . BACAGH, buk, buk . . .*'

I conducted this examination during the war, when food was short and we used to get food parcels from the United States, which for some reason always took the form of cling peaches. I don't know what the Americans thought we were suffering from—massive cling peach deficiency presumably. And one of the ways my own family was digging for victory was to rear chickens. We moved around a lot, following my father from one military hospital to another, not because he was a patient, but because he was a military psychiatrist and was often shifted from one nut-house to the next. Everywhere we went, we took a trailer behind the car, filled with hens. They would be kept in a camp at the bottom of the garden, like displaced persons. I watched these creatures for hours on end. They tormented me.

2

I offer an example of humour from my professional experience. Recently, I directed a production of Eugene O'Neill's *Long Day's Journey Into Night.* I wanted to see what would happen if I treated the play not as Greek tragedy, which is what O'Neill wanted, but as an orphan object that I had just found. And it struck me, as a foreigner, that it was a highly skilful version of a family squabble. Therefore, it seemed to me, it was necessary to get away from the usual incantatory manner of performing O'Neill and restore to the play the quality of conversation. In the process of making it like conversation something happened: it produced laughter. It was like moving a match over the abrasive surface on the box. If you move the match slowly, nothing happens, but if you strike at the right tempo—flames. There is the moment at the end of the play, when the mother comes downstairs in a demented state of morphine intoxication and the drunken elder brother turns and says, 'The mad scene, enter Ophelia.' The scene developed a momentum as we rehearsed, increasing in pace until the first preview the actor playing the part rose to his feet and said, at *terrific* speed, 'The mad scene, enter Ophelia,' and there was a roar of laughter from the audience. We had struck the match. The actor, afterwards, was devastated.

It was much earlier, in fact—while Peter Cook, Alan Bennett, Dudley Moore and myself were performing 'Beyond the Fringe'—that I became very interested in what was happening up there on the stage, what it was that produced this strange respiratory convulsion. By the thousandth performance, it sounds like a sudden explosion, a noise from another planet. I became fascinated with laughter.

I had trained as a biologist and felt that if we do something from which we get acute pleasure, like laughter, it must have been planted in us, or else we acquired it, because it has powerful selective advantage. We wouldn't, that is, have the *experience* of pleasure unless there was, for the species, some sort of selective advantage in the *behaviour* that leads to it. Which immediately raises the question: what is it that nature gets out of the pleasure we take from laughter?

There are various theories. Henri Bergson thought it was the collective criticism of some anomalous and unfruitful behaviour on the part of one member of the herd. Freud saw it as the release of tension following the sudden introduction of forbidden material into consciousness.

I prefer to think something much more comprehensive is going on when we get pleasure out of, say, hearing a joke. Jokes are of course peculiar and rather limited examples, a subset of the large domain of humour. I think that jokes are a social lubricant— sometimes a highly formulaic one—that we use for the purposes of maintaining conviviality, especially among men. Men, as soon as they are in all-male company, start telling jokes like it was some sort of convulsion. In fact, one of the more trying features of being with lots of men is that jokes break out like an illness. It's a way of both keeping one's distance and registering membership of a group when there are no spontaneous grounds for shared membership. So-and-so says, 'Have you heard the one about bum bum bum bum?' and someone else says, 'That reminds me, did you hear the one about bum bum bum bum?' and before you know where you are there's a competitive fugue of joke-telling, like the Kwakiutl Indians who throw piles of blankets and copper shields into the sea in a demonstration of competitive hospitality. Jokes are a sign that you have in your pocket a social currency that allows you to join the game.

I'm fascinated by the ritual procedure of the exchange and also the obligatory response. In only one joke out of five is that response spontaneous laughter. The rest of the time the joke-hearers feel it incumbent on themselves to contribute a skilful impersonation of being killed with laughter. You hold your sides, you slap your thighs, you say, 'Doggone.' And this is simply to maintain the joke-teller's self-esteem. It is almost impossible, unless you are insensitive or almost pathologically sadistic, to withhold the impersonation of laughter from someone who has just told you a joke.

In fact, jokes have little to do with spontaneous humour. The teller has the same relationship to them that he or she might have to a Hertz Rent-a-Car. A joke is a hired object, with many previous users, and very often its ashtrays are filled with other people's cigarettes, and its gears are worn and slipping, because other people have driven this joke very badly before you got behind the wheel.

Jokes also conform to strict patterns, one of the most common being any one of a number of jocular trinities that cruise the world: 'There was this English fellow, an Irishman and a Jewish fellow.' They have a toy mechanism which is very simple and very conventional. It would not be difficult, I suspect, to produce a taxonomy of *all* jokes. There are not many types. There is the type about the deaf, blind or disabled; the type involving different nationalities; the type that works fine as long as you assume there are people who walk the street with names like 'Fuckarada'; and the type that, while still formulaic, draws on the news. For example: the *Challenger* jokes after the Shuttle disaster, the Chicken Kiev jokes after Chernobyl.

And when you laugh at any one of these various types you're really laughing at the predictable, or rather at the strange tension that exists between predictable generalization and a specific instance of it. Take the Jack Benny joke which was on one of his radio shows. We hear footsteps coming up behind Jack Benny, and a voice saying, 'Your money or your life.' There's silence. The voice repeats, 'Your money or your life.' And there's another long gap before Benny says, 'I'm thinking.' This is a pretty good joke; it relies on a generalization familiar to the audience—Jack Benny is very mean—and it works because it is a surprising way of reacquainting the audience with the generalization. When you laugh, you're laughing at the very specific way Jack Benny has characterized himself.

I REMEMBER a sketch in 'Beyond the Fringe'. Peter Cook was a strange, rather withdrawn man in a shabby raincoat, sitting on a bench blankly asserting that he could have been a judge only he didn't have the Latin for the judging exams. He said, 'They're extremely rigorous, the judging exams, as compared to the mining exams which are extremely unrigorous, see. They only ask you one question: "What is your name?" I got seventy-five per cent on that.'

For years I tried to work out precisely why this was funny. On one level it's obvious, but there is more to it than simply the obvious. It is an instance of what a philosopher would call a category mistake: it is in the nature of names that they are not something you can have seventy-five per cent knowledge of. You either know them or you don't. The sketch makes us conscious of something we know but don't generally think about, because it occurs at a pre-attentive level. You can only be examined on subjects in which there can be a scale of success. And knowing one's name is not, actually, one of those things. Another example: a cartoon in the *New Yorker* shows two explorers up to their neck in quicksand and there are these creepers hanging down; it's quite clear they are in difficulties, and the man behind is saying to the one in front, 'Quicksand or not, Barclay, I've half a mind to struggle.' Now it is in the nature of voluntary and involuntary action that they are distinct categories of thought. What this joke makes us aware of is that it's in the nature of struggling that you can't have half a mind to do it. You don't, as it were, say, 'Right, well, we've tried firing warning shots to alert the base camp, we've tried treading water, let's give struggling a chance.' Struggling, for example, could not feature as an Olympic event.

The joke makes us aware that we have complex notions about those things for which we can be praised and blamed, those things which could be said to be voluntary or involuntary, those things which we can do half-heartedly, those things which we do flat out and those things we can't help. The joke invites a readiness to re-perceive the world.

3

Both my parents were Jewish. My mother was a reluctant and unwilling Jew, my father an embarrassed and guilty one. He was guilty because he had sprung away from his traditional orthodox ghetto background in the East End of London. His father had arrived in England in the 1870s and established a patriarchal Jewish household in Whitechapel. My father, contrary to what was expected of him, went to Cambridge University and became a doctor. Years later, after the Holocaust, he came to feel guilt about this. He felt that he had gone too far from his roots and that he owed his people a debt. He tried to redeem that debt by seeing that his own children, who had not been raised as orthodox Jews, should begin to observe. For me, all this was improvised a bit hastily and a bit late. I was taken to Synagogue or Temple, and found myself puzzled by the fact that Jews had these peculiar books that were read backwards, written in a script that was unfamiliar. The books themselves resembled sheets of scorched matzo.

My father would create these Friday-night suppers with candles and an instant décor of Judaism. I had no interest in this whatsoever. I was told constantly by my father that I owed it to my people to identify with them. I didn't know how to, and didn't want to. I could feel Jewish only for anti-Semites, not for Jews. As a child I resented being Jewish: it seemed designed just to prevent me having fun. I spent the early part of my life dreaming, not of a white Christmas, but of a White Anglo-Saxon Protestant Christmas. There was this wonderful world of jolly people and Father Christmas in brilliant scarlet, a colour which never figured in Jewish life, with a white beard and jolly red cheeks, and I felt like one of those children in Hans Christian Andersen, with my nose pressed to the frosty pane. In a sense I felt myself neither fish nor fowl nor good red herring. Nor good salt herring, I'm afraid. (All of which reminds me of *The Merchant of Venice* which I directed with Lord Olivier, who arrived at one of the first rehearsals saying, 'My dear boy, as we are about to do this difficult and awful play, we must at all costs avoid offending the Hebrews, God I love them so.' And then he proceeded to bedeck himself with very complicated and offensive facial equipment. He had this nose made for himself that was like something out of *Die Sturmer*. And ringlets. And, finally, he spent £1,500 on a pair of dentures. I kept on saying, 'Larry, please don't do that, it's awful. Not many of us are like that really, and it will create an awfully offensive effect.' It took a long time to persuade him to drop this terrible equipment, but I never could get him to abandon the dentures.)

MY MOTHER was quite a bit different from my father. She was a writer, and had published her first novel when she was nineteen. She wrote all day and every day, and was rather intolerant of the noise made by her small children. She didn't like intrusions. She battered away on this funny little typewriter. She used the same one until she died. That was what she was like. She preserved in her life a scrupulous monotony. She rose at the same time every day, sent us to school and began to tap away at the typewriter, or else noted sentences, or fragments of sentences, on the slit-open envelopes of letters she'd received that morning, a habit encouraged by the paper shortage during the war. She would put away her typewriter at twelve-thirty prompt when we came back for lunch. This would be a rather glum meal of boiled chicken, not one of the chickens we kept, but another chicken, a chicken which looked as though it had never said a single '*bacagh*' in its entire life and had been simply tipped into hot water and come out with that awful goose-pimpled appearance that boiled chickens have. We ate the same meal every day. Boiled chicken, year in, year out.

My mother was an admirer of a little-known French writer whose name was Francis Ponge, a sort of parody name. Ponge was a man after my mother's own heart. Ponge wrote in minute detail about the appearance of such things as sand and mimosa and soap. Soap particularly fascinated him. Ponge wrote long essays on the appearance of soap, page after page of descriptions of soap. He wrote a novel titled *Soap*. My mother translated some of his poetry. This also concerned soap.

My mother taught me something of which I was very impatient at the time: the value of monotony. With hindsight I see that the imposition of her routine was in effect a spiritual exercise which has lasted the rest of my life. She saw epiphanies in the mundane.

Eventually I became fascinated by the appearance of the commonplace as well. I learned the pleasure of simply watching. I take enormous pleasure from watching, in restaurants, in railway carriages or on street-corners. Anywhere. Elevators are good places. I like to see the way we handle social encounters at awkward moments. I like to see the little signs, the tiny gestures, the twitches and grimaces of embarrassment. And it is here, amid the most minute detail of the commonplace and the ordinary and the mundane, that I find the greatest displays of humour.

4

Finally, I also like to remember the noise of certain English steam trains. English steam trains which used to make a noise as they pulled out of smoky, bronchitic stations in North London. Hmmm. This is very long ago. I see myself in short trousers thinking about Betty Grable. First of all it was the whistle of the trains: '*Whoooooooooo.*' Then: '*Chkuu, chkuu, ching, chkuu, chkuu, ching, chkuu, ching, chkuu, ching, chkuu, ching, chkuu, chkuu, ching, chkuu, chkuu* (faster and faster, softening to a gentle rhythm), *chkuu, ching, ching, chkuu, chkuu, ching, chkuu, ching, chkuu, chkuu, ching, ching, chkuu, chkuu, ching.*'

And so forth.

THE EUROPEAN GAY REVIEW

Editor: Salvatore Santagati

Essays in Volume Two include

DAVID ROBINSON	**YVES NAVARRE**
Gay Images in Cinema	*The Little Rogue in our Flesh*
EDWARD LUCIE-SMITH	**JAMES KIRKUP**
Théodore Géricault	*On Mishima and Yourcenar*
TED HONDERICH	**NICHOLAS DE JONGH**
Gay Political Violence	*British Homophobia*

"A lively initiative" *(The Observer)* – "Very good, very interesting" (Iris Murdoch) – "Important" (Dominique Fernandez, Prix Goncourt). "Beautifully produced" *(The New Statesman)*

Book-format, illustrated pp.144. To obtain single copy please send £5.95 (UK), £8, US $14 (rest of world, airmail) P&P incl to EGR, BCM Box 8970, London WC1N 3XX, England. Subscription (4 Vols): £24 (UK), £32 (outside), US $55. Libraries: £40, US $65.

NICHOLAS
SHAKESPEARE
IN PURSUIT OF
GUZMÁN

Lima

I arrived in Lima, having forgotten what a vile city it is.

I arrived in the middle of a police strike, and the streets were crowded with hooded officers. They were shooting guns in the air, and some had commandeered buses. They were protesting against a regulation requiring them to supply their own uniforms and practice ammunition. They held aloft their symbol, a worn-out boot.

That night I counted seventeen explosions—not from the police but from guerrillas. The next evening the restaurant around around the corner was machine-gunned and then blown up with dynamite. There was a curfew, and each morning I discovered new graffiti on the walls, slogans painted in red celebrating the guerrillas, Sendero Luminoso, the 'Shining Path'. The slogans also celebrated the man who led Sendero. They called him *Presidente* Gonzalo, but his name was Abimael Guzmán. I had come to Lima to find Guzmán, although I knew I wouldn't succeed. I didn't. But that was the reason I was here.

In fact, Guzmán hadn't been spotted since 1981, and not much was known about him. He had been pictured with a Devil's tail: they said he taught his young initiates to murder and then forced them to drink the blood of their victims. They said he was in league with drug-traffickers, that he was dying or that he was dead or that he was abroad—in Bolivia, New York, London. I read one newspaper with the headline, 'ABIMAEL VISITS HARRODS?'

For that matter, not much was known about his followers, the Senderistas. They gave no interviews, issued few statements and did not claim responsibility for their bombings. They accepted no funds from abroad; their weapons were stolen or hand-made: beer-can bombs hurled from slings made of llama hair. Most people believed their story began eight years ago in the village of Chuschi.

Eight years ago, in 1980, Peru held the presidential election that returned Fernando Belaúnde. Belaúnde had been removed twelve years before: in October 1968, the military had entered the presidential palace through a guard-room lavatory and carried him out, still wearing his pyjamas. On his return,

Opposite: Abimael Guzmán

151

Belaúnde found plenty of unfinished business—the single achievement of his previous Minister of Agriculture had been to sign a permit allowing a dog into the country—and the events in a little Andean village went unnoticed.

Chuschi is near a source of the Amazon. Three hundred families live there, growing maize on the terraces overlooking the Río Pampas Valley and tending a few animals. Once a year the priest succeeds in getting members of the village to clean out the irrigation ditches; occasionally, they tidy the church. On 18 May 1980, the day of Peru's elections, the village of Chuschi was visited by strangers. They had come to burn the ballot boxes. 'The old dead-end votes,' the visitors announced, served only to preserve the old order. 'A new path of arms' would lead Peru towards a transformed society that served the people.

The date of the ballot-burning was interesting. Peru's last great Indian revolt was nearly 200 years before led by a man named José Gabriel Condorcanqui who called himself the Inca Túpac Amaru II. He wore his hair long, in ringlets, and carried a grey blunderbuss with a mouth the size of an orange. He was captured by the Spanish in Cuzco in 1781 and was led to the main square where his tongue was cut out, and his body was pulled apart by horses. His limbs were then packed in leather bags and sent by mule for exhibition in the provinces of Chumbivilcas, Lampa and Carabaya. But there was a legend among Peruvian Indians that José Gabriel Condorcanqui did not die in 1781, and that his limbs were re-growing underground. One day, it was believed, the pieces of his body would be joined together, and Inca Túpac Amaru II would rise up to liberate his people.

Inca Túpac Amaru II was executed on 18 May 1781. It was the same day, 199 years later, 18 May 1980, that Sendero arrived in Chuschi, bearing, for the first time, the news of President Gonzalo.

About two months after the ballot-burning, on Independence Day, dynamite was thrown into the ranks of a procession in Ayacucho—the 'capital' of the Andes—and an army captain trod out the fuse. The next day, in the city of Arequipa, 275 miles south of Ayacucho, an electricity pylon was blown up, and the city was left without light. In August, there were nineteen different bombings, finally prompting a statement from the Minister of the Interior: there were no guerrillas in Peru, but there appeared to be a problem with 'delinquents'.

In the following month, September, delinquents seized 2,000 sticks of dynamite from a mine in Huancayo. On 5 November, twenty delinquents invaded the town of Vischongo, and raised a red flag in the square. On 23 December, in San Agustín de Ayzcara, a land-owner was killed. Three days later, the day after Christmas, delinquents had hung dead dogs from the traffic lights in Lima, with dynamite stuffed in their mouths and placards tied round their necks identifying them as the Chinese leader Deng Xiaoping, whose 'fascist dictatorship' had betrayed the world revolution. It was a mystifying spectacle. Leaflets explained that a dead dog was the Indian symbol of a tyrant condemned to death by his people.

The government was unconcerned; 'narco-terrorists', according to Belaúnde: there was no need for alarm; after all, he had experience with terrorists, including his successful containing of the Castro-inspired revolt of Luis de la Puente and Hector Bejar in 1965. In this instance, however, the terrorists had no identifiable leaders and no manifesto, only their own head of state: *Presidente Gonzalo.*

Finally, in early June 1981, the Minister of the Interior announced a 'decisive battle' had broken out between police and what was finally acknowledged to be the 'Shining Path'.

But the attacks continued.

Sendero had grown so sophisticated that it was able to subject Lima to a complete electrical black-out on New Year's Eve or during the Pope's visit: the only light came from the hills across the city, where huge bonfires burned in the shape of the hammer and sickle. One day saw the bombing of the American Embassy and the Chinese Embassy ('Dogs who betrayed the Cultural Revolution') and the Indian Embassy and the embassies of Italy and Chile and the Cultural Centre of the Soviet Union ('Filthy Revisionists'). There was a joke. Only two things worked in Peru: the women's volley-ball team and Sendero Luminoso.

And still the attacks continued—in Ayacucho, dogs ran through the streets with bombs strapped to their backs; in a market crowd at Huanta, a donkey exploded; in Lima's Crillón Hotel, a

Nicholas Shakespeare

child walked into the foyer and blew up; in Chimbote a telephone exchange was damaged by an explosive attached to a duck—until finally, on 29 December, Belaúnde finally declared a state of emergency in the three Andean regions of Ayacucho, Huancavelica and Apurímac.

Suddenly in Ayacucho soldiers were seen in the streets wearing round their necks the mutilated corpses of dogs. In Chuschi, a soldier fixed a stick of dynamite to a peasant, noting afterwards that, 'This is how terrorists die.' In Soccos thirty-four villagers were machine-gunned and then set alight with incendiary grenades. One survivor lay in a hole beside her husband, watching him burn 'like a roast pig'.

Belaúnde did not stand in the elections of 1985.

Belaúnde's successor was Alan García, thirty-seven years old, head of the American Popular Revolutionary Alliance. García had been elected, confident that his centre-leftist policies would appease the Senderistas. He was wrong. They saw him as just another bourgeois politician. By the end of 1987, Sendero assassins were killing an average of four officials each day. Military intelligence maps revealed that Sendero could launch assaults at any point along the spine of the Andes, from Jaen in the north to Puno in the south. Several areas of the Upper Huallaga, where Sendero had reportedly come to an understanding with the region's drugs-traffickers, had simply passed out of government control. Over 11,000 people had been killed. García himself had nearly died, once in a mortar attack and once when an old peasant woman pushed forward to embrace him, concealing several sticks of dynamite beneath her skirt.

In May 1987, García offered a reward of $80,000 to anyone whose efforts would lead to the arrest of Julio Mezzich, Osman Morote, and, the most wanted of all, Abimael Guzmán.

When I arrived in Lima last summer, I discovered at least five journalists writing books on Sendero, among them Manuel Granados, formerly a student at the university at Ayacucho. His bachelor's thesis, completed eight years ago, was a study of Sendero's early history—perhaps the most thorough study

Opposite: Illustration from Sendero communiqué, 1987.

¡VIVA LA LUCHA ARMADA!

if only because Granados knew personally the people he was writing about.

But there were only three copies of Granados's thesis, and on seeing one I understood why there were no more. At the time, Granados said, Sendero 'seemed to have no future, and I criticized everything they were doing in Ayacucho.' He criticized Sendero to such an extent that the three professors assigned to mark his thesis all resigned. The next three nominations also refused. Sendero had an effect on people, and Granados was warned that his thesis would be held against him, 'when the time comes to send me to Heaven.' Granados's nails had been bitten down, and, throughout our meeting, his eyes moved constantly, flicking, flicking. It was the first time I had seen this kind of nervousness. Later I would see it frequently.

Granados pointed out that the full name was not Sendero Luminoso, the 'Shining Path', but the 'Peruvian Communist Party for the Shining Path of José Carlos Mariátegui'. Mariátegui, a morose cripple with a falsetto voice, was the founder of the Peruvian Socialist Party in the twenties. Like many of his subsequent Sendero followers, Mariátegui had hoped to become a priest—the Roman Catholic Church remains the only institution left untroubled in Peru—but ended up as a journalist, his most influential work being the polemical *Seven Interpretive Essays on Peruvian Reality*. In this, his followers claimed, he became the first to understand the reality of Peruvian society: that it was a land of Indians whose position as underdogs had remained unchanged since Pizarro's Conquest. The Spanish had destroyed an impressive society—the Incas—and had not replaced it, and for Mariátegui and his disciples the pre-Conquest Inca empire of Twantinsuyo represented a kind of primitive communist society. The future would combine revolutionary Marxism with the society of the Incas.

Like Mariátegui, who described Peru as a 'semi-feudal and semi-colonial country', Senderistas saw around them the same conditions that characterized China before Mao. They hoped, in following Mariátegui's Shining Path, to introduce the thoughts of Chairman Mao to a Peru of the Incas, and arrive at a New Democracy.

The proponent of the 'New Democracy', Abimael Guzmán, was born, illegitimate, on 4 December 1934—an anniversary regularly commemorated by Sendero in Lima with a black-out. He was born with the Old Testament name of his father, Abismael, later dropping the letter 's' to assume the name of one of the Horsemen of the Apocalypse.

The Guzmán family doctor lived in Lima in a house near the sea, and, although now eighty-nine, he remembered Abimael's father as a small, square man who didn't drink or dance. His weakness was women. Sometimes he had three at the same time. One of them was Abimael's mother, Berenice Reynoso. After Abimael's birth, his father moved to Mollendo, a port fifteen miles away. The doctor said, 'He had a shop on the corner of Arequipa in front of the market where he sold rice and sugar. He lived above it with his "official" woman—a Chilean. She was a better class of woman than Abimael's mother.'

But Berenice Reynoso followed, also moving to Mollendo and living with her son 150 yards away in a yellow-wood house consisting of two rooms and a patio where they cooked. The father visited at night. When his mother died in 1939, Abimael, the bastard, was moved in with his Chilean step-mother. A picture was starting to emerge. I decided to fly south to Arequipa, about 450 miles, to the town where Guzmán grew up.

Arequipa

Arequipa is one of the most dramatic cities in Peru. Its buildings are made of white stone, and the snow-capped volcano Misti can be seen from every street. It was here that Guzmán attended secondary school. I spent several days in Arequipa. While there, I met by chance a man who had been at the the same school at the same time. When I mentioned Guzmán's name, however, the class-mate showed the familiar apprehensions: Guzmán, he assured me, would kill him if his name was known.

I promised several times not to reveal it, but nothing I said seemed to help. He was terrified.

'*Es un loco*,' he repeated, '*un loco*.'

Slowly some details emerged.

For instance, I learned that Guzmán had won a prize for *good* conduct. It wasn't much, admittedly. I learned that Guzmán was religious—'very religious'—introspective, and virtually impenetrable. I learned that he never drank, never went to parties, never played games, never had girl-friends. 'None of us,' the class-mate said, 'could ever have imagined that Guzmán would grow up to be what he is now: Peru's most wanted assassin.'

The class-mate opened a school magazine from 1952, which included reports on each student's performance. Guzmán was not exceptional and I saw little to support the myth surrounding him— of the genius whose childhood was spent exclusively with books. He was, in almost every respect, average, distinguishing himself in only Spanish and the history of Peru. The 1952 report also showed his mug-shot: handsome, with gleaming hair and dark, blank eyes. He looked like a dandy, Spanish rather than Indian.

I looked at the picture for some time, and then flipped through the pages until I came across a mention of Guzmán and then an article by him. His first words in print, an account of how Guzmán had succeeded in organizing students into a number of extra-curricular groups devoted to the study of culture, sport, religion, journalism and economics. 'At the head of each group there will be a leader. The group leader will appoint four assistants . . . there will be a central committee made up of nine members.'

It was not much, but its logic had an appeal: Guzmán, at seventeen, already organizing.

I asked the class-mate if he could remember anything else about Guzmán—a detail, an event.

'No. No incidents. He was . . . he was—' he said, shaking his head, searching for the appropriate word, 'he was an *anonymity*.'

In the following year, 1953, Guzmán would have been nineteen, about the time he dropped the 's' from his Christian name and went to Arequipa's University of San Agustín, where he studied philosophy and law. I learned that the current rector was in fact Guzmán's former teacher. I got an appointment by mentioning a mutual acquaintance in Lima, and the Rector was delighted to see

Map: Peter Covill

PERU

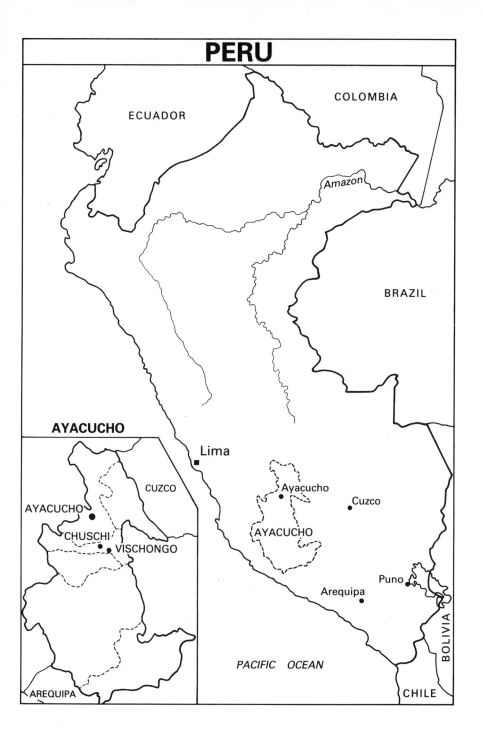

ECUADOR

COLOMBIA

Amazon

BRAZIL

AYACUCHO

Lima

CUZCO

AYACUCHO

CHUSCHI

VISCHONGO

Ayacucho

Cuzco

AYACUCHO

Puno

Arequipa

AREQUIPA

PACIFIC OCEAN

BOLIVIA

CHILE

me, until I mentioned Guzmán's name and his face suddenly went flat. It was, again, the fear. It was difficult to get him to resume talking.

Could he remember anything about Guzmán?

He could remember that Guzmán was one of his best students.

I see. Perhaps some detail? His character?

A long pause. 'Yes. Guzmán was quiet.'

Quiet?

'Yes, very quiet.'

I see.

'He was not fiery, not at all. He was not an original thinker.' And again: 'It would have been hard to believe that he wanted to change the processes of history.'

And so we sat.

'Perhaps,' the Rector said, finally, rising from his chair, 'perhaps, you should see Dr Garaycochea. Yes, it's Dr Garaycochea whom you should see.'

D r Walter Garaycochea lived on the other side of town, and so, following the Rector's advice, I made an appointment. Garaycochea was a lecturer in philosophy, and the buildings nearby were sprayed with crimson graffiti, accusing the García government of fascism and genocide. Garaycochea was remarkably forthcoming.

Garaycochea met Guzmán in 1953, the year he began studying at the university. Together they founded an institution to promote 'cultural activities', a group that met every Saturday to talk about Kant, Heidegger, Hegel, Russell, Husserl. The group also started a magazine, *Hombre y Mundo* (**Mankind** and the World), but it collapsed after three issues, and Guzmán's contribution to it was one article, a review of Pascual Jordán's *Physics in the Twentieth Century*. It was unexceptional stuff—as was true of most of Guzmán's contributions to the group. Being the youngest, he spoke the least. 'He heard everything but he didn't participate.'

I urged Garaycochea to remember something further about Guzmán, something more revealing—a detail, an incident. I asked Garaycochea, in short, the same question I had asked everyone else who knew Guzmán.

160

Nothing.

Then, suddenly, he remembered something—in fact, a story.

The event took place in 1959. Garaycochea and Guzmán had gone to a party, a graduation party given by Páquita Valladores. 'At about ten p.m. Abimael and I left the party and we went to a bar. At the bar we drank a lot. This was rare because Abimael hardly ever drank. We then went to another bar in Alto de la Luna on the other side of the market, where we talked until six in the morning.'

Dr Garaycochea looked pleased.

But what did you talk about?

Dr Garaycochea scratched his head. 'I don't know.'

Then suddenly, Dr Garaycochea grew animated again. There was another story—he was able to remember another incident. Perhaps it would help.

This was the story: 'Guzmán once went with my wife and me to see the film of *Porgy and Bess*. Afterwards we visited the Café Paris in Mercedares where we praised the film and said how lovely Gershwin's music was. Abimael disagreed. "It's a primitive film," he said. "The Americans don't understand the first thing about music." '

There was a pause.

'I see,' I said, 'that is what you remember Guzmán to have said.'

'Yes,' Dr Garaycochea said, 'about Gershwin.' He looked pleased.

Garaycochea had been one of the five men marking Guzmán's first dissertation in January 1961, a work on the Kantian theory of space. 'I think it's slightly elementary,' said Garaycochea.

It must have been original in some way. It is popularly held to be outstanding.

'Not at all. Really, it's quite remarkable that he was destined to be a political leader.'

I decided the next morning to read Guzmán's dissertation, and discovered that a copy, bound in grey, was locked in a cabinet in the Faculty of Letters. To borrow it, I had to leave my passport.

'So many people try to steal it,' said the librarian. The 178-page

essay was dedicated to Dr Miguel Angel Rodríguez Rivas. Dr
Garaycochea had spoken a great deal about Rivas. He had been the
leader of the weekly philosophy group. According to Garaycochea,
Rivas, a Marxist, was an imposing man and an attractive orator, and
he described him as Guzmán's mentor. On the dedication page,
Guzmán himself describes Rivas as 'dear friend and master'.

Guzmán's thesis consists of thirty-seven conclusions arguing
that Kant's theory of space has been superseded by advances in
modern physics. I had reached conclusion twenty-seven (a), when
the librarian leaned over, put his hands on my desk, and told me
that he had run into Guzmán in Puno in 1964.

Was I interested?

Of course.

It was, the librarian said sitting down, rather peculiar. 'I
couldn't understand why he was there.'

I asked him to explain.

Guzmán had been on a honeymoon—in the Andes. On
meeting the librarian, Guzmán introduced him to his new wife.

'But why are you in Puno?' the librarian had asked again: it was
so cold there.

Guzmán had replied: 'In Peru there's much to know and much
to do. I want to know this part of Peru because I won't have another
chance.' The librarian remembered him saying just those words,
whereupon he asked Guzmán to join him for a glass of beer.
Guzmán accepted only a mineral water.

I thanked the librarian and left, feeling increasingly frustrated.
I was not sure what I expected to find of Guzmán. I knew, however,
that I had expected more than a pedestrian autodidact who drank
mineral water on his honeymoon and whose only distinguishing
feature was a dislike for *Porgy and Bess*.

I wandered over to one of Guzmán's old haunts, La Dalmacía
in San Juan de Dios, and ordered a beer, and sat reading through
some of the material I had accumulated. In one magazine there was
a mention of a song that Guzmán liked to sing to himself: '*Pepito de
mi Corazón*'—Little Pepe of my Heart.

I tried several record shops. No one had heard the song, but, in
one, I met a man and his wife who hummed what they thought were

Opposite: Guzmán as depicted on posters by the Peruvian
armed forces (above) and Sendero.

¡BUSCADO,
COBARDE DELINCUENTE
SUBVERSIVO!

¡ENTREGALO!

the opening lines. They couldn't remember the rest. The man was a Christadelphian who believed in the pure Gospel of the first century. He promised to send me the lyrics.

The lyrics of *Pepito de mi Corazón* arrived a few weeks later.

> *Ay, Pepito, yo te ruego,*
> *Si, si, si, si es que aún me quieres*
> *Como yo te quiero. Ven hacia mi,*
> *Pepito de mi corazón.*

> (Oh, my little Pepe, I beg you,
> If, if, if, if you still love me
> As I love you. Come to me,
> Little Pepe of my heart.)

I read them and imagined the young Kantian philosopher after a night at the Dalmacía, drinking mineral water. Afterwards he would walk home through the streets of Arequipa, looking at the cloudless sky and humming the refrain of his favourite song: 'Oh, my little Pepe, I beg you—'

The morning I left I walked down the Calle Ejericios, where Guzmán had lived in Arequipa. His father, that industrious womanizer, must have come up in the world to move his family into number 307. It was a large, old, elegant house. Fine wrought-iron grilles protected the windows. Two secretaries worked in the front office. They had never heard of Guzmán. The building, they explained, was now used as a primary and secondary school: the College of the Divine Master.

Lima

I returned to Lima to meet Guzmán's 'dear friend and master', Dr Miguel Angel Rodríguez Rivas, and found the city recovering from the first anniversary of the prison massacres.

The year before, after a night of rioting, 257 suspected members of Sendero Luminoso had been killed in the prisons at Lurigancho, El Frontón and Santa Bárbara. A nun who had heard the shooting told me it was like the popping of grilled maize. Those responsible for the killing, led by the megaphone-wielding Brigadier Rabanal Portilla, had been given total, albeit unwritten, authority to crush the riot. President García had promised: 'Either all the culprits go or I go.' They remain unpunished. At three p.m. on the afternoon of the anniversary, a Friday, the Minister of the Interior appeared on television and alerted the nation to expect Sendero attacks that night. By late afternoon the city was dead. It turned out to be one of the few nights of the year when nothing happened. Sendero had none the less brought the country to a standstill.

I met Rivas in a garden where there was a parrot that shrieked at the mention of 'Mao'.

Rivas and Guzmán had been friends since the fifties. Following the earthquake in 1960, Rivas had organized a group of 200 to take an inventory of the damage. Guzmán led one of the teams. He entered the barrios—possibly for the first time—and the misery he saw had a profound effect. One evening Guzmán returned to report on a house near the Bolognesi bridge. The family lived in cold, horrible conditions, without help from the authorities, with no hope of work. 'He said only an organized people could do something, and he saw the necessity of organizing them,' Rivas remembered.

Rivas last saw his former pupil in Lima in 1972. They had talked about Mao [the parrot shrieked] and of Ayacucho, where Guzmán had gone to teach. Guzmán spoke of his intention to start a subversive movement, one that, according to Rivas, was different from the terrorist groups of Argentina or Colombia. 'Sendero,' he said, 'is an ethnic, cultural movement, señor. It recognizes that we are a fundamentally Indian republic with a fundamentally Indian outlook. It will win and its triumph will be its death and it will disappear. It will win because it is fighting an unlosable war.'

Was Guzmán alive?

'Yes,' Rivas said, without hesitation. He mentioned a pamphlet that had appeared in his office a year ago, written in a style and advancing an argument that could only be Guzmán's. The pamphlet, entitled 'Develop the People's War To Serve The World Revolution', 110 pages long, commemorates the six-year struggle. It draws on Mao and Mariátegui, and charts the progress since the burning of the ballot boxes at Chuschi: it describes how, guns in hand, the poor peasants of Peru are now about to storm the heavens, bringing about a new dawn, 'towards which fifteen billion years of matter . . . have been inevitably and irresistibly heading.' It makes, it must be admitted, for rather turgid reading. And it ends, finally, with a detailed catalogue of the atrocities allegedly committed by the armed forces. The last words are 'Long Live Chairman Gonzalo'.

Rivas had been living in Lima since 1961, when he had to leave Arequipa owing to a political dispute at the university. Following Rivas's departure, Guzmán appears to have been isolated, unable to secure a university post. It was finally Dr Efraín Morote Best, rector of the newly re-opened University of San Cristóbal de Huamanga in Ayacucho, who offered a good position to anyone from Rivas's group who was prepared to go to Ayacucho. In 1962, Guzmán had accepted.

For the Spanish-speaking Limeños, Ayacucho is part of a region referred to as *La Mancha India*, the Indian Stain. Its population of Quechua-speaking Indians has long been ignored by the central government. Life expectancy is forty-five years, with most of the population surviving barely above subsistence level. The annual income is fifty dollars, roughly the price of a Peruvian passport. In Quechua, Ayacucho means 'Corner of the Dead'.

Ayacucho

There are thirty-three churches in Ayacucho, most of them padlocked. The new buildings are the barracks near the airport. At night you can hear soldiers splashing in a pool with the prostitutes. Ayacucho is not listed in the tourist brochures. And while there are fewer bombings than before, the army is in control, and outsiders, especially journalists, are mistrusted. Journalists have been killed in Ayacucho.

I told the officer at the airport that I was a tourist.

Leaving, I was uncomfortable. No one looked at me. Women giggled as I passed. Somebody said something. And later I heard the same thing again. And again. At last I realized what they were saying: '*pistaco*'.

Photos opposite and on following six pages: Lisa Limer

I ordered a meal in a café. The chicken was lukewarm and cooked in lumpy black grease. I left a large tip and as I walked away the cook appeared from the kitchen. He spat and said, '*Pistaco*'.

I climbed into the back of a pick-up to get a lift into town. 'Let the *pistaco* walk,' said a woman.

Another woman, with gold teeth and a pony-tail like a string of garlic, pointed at the ink spots on my jacket where a pen had run. 'Indian blood,' she said and pushed her hand inside my jacket. She said she was looking for a knife.

Pistaco.

In the local paper *Ahora!*, I read an article, 'Ayacucho lives in terror', and from it I learned that a *pistaco* was a tall white foreigner who slept by day, drank a lot of milk and carried a long white knife under his coat. He used the knife to cut up Indians. He chopped off heads and limbs, and kept their trunks for the human grease with which he oiled his machines. Europe's industrial revolution had been lubricated with the lard made from helpless Indians. So had been the Vietnam and Korean wars. The space shuttle Challenger, I learned, had blown up because it lacked this '*aceite humano*'.

Another word for *pistaco* is *nakaq*, which comes from the Quechua *nakay*, to strangle, and references to it occurred as early as 1571. I discovered a paper on the subject written in 1951 by Dr Morote in which he lists the *pistaco*'s characteristics:

1. He is semi-human, wild and cruel.
2. He lives alone in inaccessible places.
3. He is white or mestizo with a long beard, dishevelled hair and a fearsome face.
4. His weapons are a knife and a lasso made from human skin.
5. He waits on roads and bridges.
6. He attacks by night.
7. He strangles.
8. He extracts human grease.
9. He makes his victims disappear.
10. He uses the grease to melt down bells.
11. He is mortal. He has one son who takes his place when he dies.

Opposite: *Campesinos* or peasant militiamen in Ayacucho Province.

Preceding two pages: Unearthing of the bodies of eleven people massacred on the outskirts of Ayacucho in 1983.

Photos opposite and on preceding four pages: Vera Lentz (Impact)

I had a long conversation with a grim man wearing a Coca-Cola baseball cap. *Pistacos*, he told me, had recently hacked the limbs off 30,000 Indians.

I said I was a little sceptical. Had he any evidence?

Oh, no, but he'd seen it in the press. Most *pistacos* were government mercenaries employed by President García to pay off his $15 billion debt. The blood he sold to the blood banks, the oil to western industry. The man thought García's *pistacos* were Argentinian.

But he is wrong, a taxi-driver told me later. They were not Argentinian. They were Swiss.

No, insisted another, later that same day. They came from Cangallo, two hours away.

At night, there were large groups walking the streets, blowing whistles, thumping pan lids, pushing lanterns into the face of anyone they met, convinced their children were in danger. I had heard what had happened to the last white man to visit Ayacucho, two weeks before. He was Luis Angel Calderón, who, after returning from a brothel in the Avenida Cuzco, was set upon by a crowd. Luis Calderón's head was crushed by stones, because you cannot shoot a *pistaco*, and his eyes were pulled out by hand. His body was then dragged through the Victoria district until the bones showed. Luis Calderón had been a commercial traveller from Huancayo.

A lecturer from the university told me that some believed the *pistaco* myth had been revived by Sendero to make things difficult for the army. He argued that the myth was the Indian way of explaining the Spanish domination, and that the present manifestation was not organized but spontaneous: the community, under fire from both the military and Sendero, had turned against all.

I had sought out the lecturer, hoping he would illustrate the extent of Sendero's influence in Ayacucho. I made him uncomfortable, because people were always uncomfortable whenever Sendero was mentioned and also because I was white: many of his colleagues at the university believed the *pistaco* myth. He invited me that evening to see a film of the funeral of Edith Lagos. She was the Ayacucho regional chief—nineteen years old, with long dark hair and a convent education—who died 'heroically in battle' in 1982.

The lecturer explained. 'Twice we were told she was dead and she wasn't. The third time no one believed it, so the government said the body had to be displayed.' The film showed a crowd of 30,000, so tightly packed the people had to clap with hands above their heads. The coffin moved out of the cathedral and someone arranged a red flag on the coffin. The flag bore a hammer and sickle.

'The armed people will win!' shouted the mourners. 'The people will never forget spilled blood.'

'Who killed her?'

'Belaúnde!'

'Who will avenge her?'

'The people!' roared the crowd.

The lecturer said this was the Robin Hood phase for Sendero: more people turned up for Lagos's funeral than for the Pope's visit. The film jumped to the house of Edith Lagos's parents, where medical students were examining the body. They discovered a bullet near the kidney and a knife thrust in the pelvis. Her bloody shirt was held to the camera.

I walked to the cemetery on the outskirts of the town. I met the boy who painted the names on the headstones. He showed me the headstone of Luis Angel Calderón, the *pistaco*; there was only one date, 10 September 1987. He took me to Lagos's tomb, where there was a vase of yellow and red roses. The boy asked my name. I told him.

'Hamlet,' he said. He knew the grave-digger's scene. He told me about Edith Lagos's burial. Sendero had been there with guns. So had *Presidente* Gonzalo. 'I didn't know it was him till I saw his photo in a newspaper a few days later.'

I met two white priests who had worked around Ayacucho for twenty years. They belonged to a denomination founded by a Boston cardinal determined to save South America from communism. 'Lima only starts caring about the Indians when the food is spoiling in the freezer,' said one, who had a frizzy scrub of hair and smoked a black pipe.

'Round here, there's one doctor for every 39,000 people. About fifty per cent of all children die before the age of five—and it's getting worse. The people are Stone Age up here. They sit in a field watching a cow. That's what they do all day. I used to think they were contemplative. In fact they're so lacking in self-awareness that I'm sure they find it difficult to distinguish between themselves and their environment. There is no point talking about political consciousness, about Mao or Mariátegui; they wouldn't have a clue. They don't know what's going on.'

In 1985 the priest had asked one of the men working in his church how he was going to vote. 'Belaúnde,' said the man, because Belaúnde was a '*muy bien caballero*'. Belaúnde wasn't even standing.

'They're so simple it's unbelievable,' the priest went on. 'They've never seen newspapers. They don't know where Lima is. If they do go to Lima, they're never seen again. The move from *campo* to city has been compared to moving from the age of the Pharaohs to modern New York in four days. That's the length of their bus journey. And yet the strange thing about Sendero is that they don't make any attempt to woo these people. They'll even slaughter their animals—which is anathema to the campesinos. The animals are all they've got. They can't even afford to eat them.'

The other priest began to talk. He had a beard and his neck was burnt red by the sun. He said, 'Sendero will arrive one day. They'll pick up someone in the outskirts and ask who the authorities are. I'm not talking about powerful vested interests but a piddling little town of 200 people and the guy who maintains the church. To save ammunition they then crush him with rocks. I saw two kids who'd been killed in this way. You couldn't tell one from the other. Their mother identified them by their clothes.'

'Tell him about Cabana,' said the one with the pipe.

'Cabana,' said the other. 'A town of 220 people. Sendero arrived at five in the afternoon. They herded the authorities into the square—a grassy area with a school and a playing field. They lined them up inside the goal-posts. The mayor, the magistrate, the government representative, the chap who held the key to the graveyard. Six altogether. Their heads were jerked back by the hair and their throats were cut like chickens. It was a teenage girl doing it. She was the leader. She held a bucket beneath their necks to collect the blood. It was used to daub communist slogans on the walls. Their feet and heads were then cut off and sewn on backwards.

'It's an Andean tradition. The heads, so the dead won't recognize you; the feet, so they won't follow. Not that Sendero need worry. Nobody will talk. No one will give away any information at all. It's not called terrorism for nothing.'

This was not the first time I had heard about Sendero's women leaders. I asked about Edith Lagos. According to the bearded priest, Edith Lagos was being taught to drive by her common-law husband; needing a vehicle for the lesson, they stole a truck, but the truck developed engine trouble. About that time, another truck appeared, coming round the corner, which they both felt was more suitable for finishing the lesson. The other truck was being driven by prison police, on their way to Ocobamba in seach of an escaped prisoner. They opened fire and Lagos was killed. Her body was dragged away by her companion and hidden. A child who witnessed this told the police who took it into the hospital in Andahuaylas. A finger-tip was cut off and sent to Lima for prints. Meanwhile the body lay for two days without anyone claiming it.

'She had been living in the rough for so long that her hair was riddled with lice. Eventually a social worker called on me to say they wanted to get the body out of the morgue. No one was going to claim it.'

Huanta

From Ayacucho, Huanta was a three-hour drive through the mountains. Some of the most extreme violence in the war between Sendero and the armed forces had taken place here. I travelled there on the flatbed of a truck. My companions were women. It was a curious journey. I could not hear entire conversations, but I could hear phrases, parts of sentences. '*Pistaco*,' I heard again, first from children by the roadside and later a woman in the truck, although by the time we arrived she was smiling. I heard 'PIP', the word for the plain clothes police, and I heard the broken details of a machete killing committed by Sendero. There was mention of women disappearing and a child taken from the streets.

I had travelled to Huanta because it was the day of the great regional fair. In the past Sendero had actively discouraged these traditional *ferias*, arguing that they fed the urban capitalist system at a time when it must be starved, though for the really poor the fairs remained the only chance to earn money for paraffin and salt. This time, the night before the fair, Sendero had attacked the town with dynamite, and there were soldiers everywhere. They sat in Jeeps and open trucks. They stood at street corners in black tunics with yellow skulls on their shoulders. They strolled through the crowds of people who pretended not to notice and instead played hula-hoop for prizes of Carnation Milk.

A procession began. There were red velvet banners, a bad brass band and the cross of Our Lord of Mainay. There were dancers and a man with a red violin. In one dance, the dancers wore masks and pith helmets representing Spanish overlords. Another dance was quite different and featured a man in an orange cap and green jacket, carrying a plastic machine-gun that he jabbed into the backs of five men with painted black faces, who cowered, then approached, and all at once rushed and tossed him into the air.

'Sendero!'

And the following day they attacked.

The bingo announcer appealed for calm, and the crowd scattered, leaving behind the corpse of a nineteen-year-old soldier. A twelve-year-old boy was wounded in the cross-fire, and you could hear his crying.

I caught a pick-up back to Ayacucho along with two young boys. Ten miles out of Huanta the vehicle was flagged down by ten men in ponchos, their faces covered by black Balaclavas, except that of the leader, who wore a camouflage cowboy hat. One carried a cassette recorder. All had guns. They were not interested in me. Instead they crowded round the youngest boy and began a fierce interrogation. He was wearing a blue track-suit and could not have been more than nine, the age that Sendero begin recruiting. I heard their questions.

'Who are you?'

'Where are you from?'

'Where are you going?'

The boy answered with remarkable calm, and the man in the cowboy hat hammered the roof of the truck and led his men down.

'Gracias,' shouted the driver, ironically.

The men filed up a narrow path on the dry hill and disappeared among the paddle-shaped cacti. They were members of a military intelligence unit, and I assumed they were operating from Huanta, the main base in the area.

Later I met a former member of one of the intelligence units, an articulate, well-dressed and mild man, who described how the units worked, trapping the Senderistas while they recruited from the villages. 'Collaborators in the villages would inform us that a meeting was to be held at such and such a time and place, and we would drive part of the way and walk the rest until we reached the house where the meeting was taking place, which we would then surround and ask those inside to come out with their hands up. If they began firing, we fired back, usually with grenades.'

He said that he personally had killed five people. He had been taught to kill with a knife, he said, so people would believe that the killing had been done by Sendero. 'It was common to convince them that they'd be freed if they told us everything, and afterwards we'd escort them to their homes, and along the way, usually in open country, we'd kill them. It was easier this way. After all, it's a war. They were campesinos. They didn't know why they were fighting.'

What did the people think of Abimael Guzmán?

'They thought he and Mao were liberators—like San Martín and Bolognesi—who were fighting to make the country free.' Although the Peruvian military had used less brutal tactics (for instance, General Huamán's 'Hearts and Minds Campaign' in 1984), the young man's views were shared by many others—shared for instance by the senior air force officer I met later at a reception in Lima: 'The Argentine solution,' he whispered approvingly. 'Go in and kill them. When an apple has a rotten core, cut it out.' He leaned closer. 'Everyone knows who they are. It's only the law which prevents us from solving the problem.'

Ayacucho

When I returned to Ayacucho, the cocks, for reasons no one understood, were crowing relentlessly. They sounded like dogs howling. On my return, I intended to visit Guzmán's old house on Calle Libertad, and had an introduction to see Juan Granda, the professor who now lived there.

Walking there, I passed a row of old women, sitting in the shade beside heaps of coca leaves, who hissed at me as I went by.

Guzmán would have arrived here twenty-four years ago, one year before the city's first telephone was installed. Ayacucho would have seemed remote, provincial. Yet it is in the urban centres that thought evaporates; there are too many distractions. In a place like Ayacucho you can go to bed with a book by a lamp that then goes out. You are cut off; your thoughts become more extreme and, if put into action, more effective. Kant, the subject of Guzmán's thesis, had constructed an elaborate metaphysical critique while rarely leaving Koenigsberg.

Guzmán worked initially in the Faculty of Social Sciences. Following the Sino-Soviet split in 1964, Guzmán turned from Stalinism to Maoism—a realignment which explains his lukewarm attitude to Peru's Castro-inspired uprisings in 1965 (Che Guevara 'was a chorus girl'). In the same year he married one of his pupils, Augusta de la Torre, the middle-class daughter of local left-wing activists who introduced him to a network of contacts in the region. One person who knew her described Augusta as a militant with a nice figure: 'She was small, like him, and *absolutamente seria*. She didn't respond or acknowledge your presence—ever. It was as if you were nothing.'

In January 1965, Guzmán made the first of three visits to China.

Most of Sendero's leadership and support came from the classrooms of San Cristóbal de Huamanga, from provincial academics who had little in common with the *serranos* from the mountains and did not even speak Quechua. By the 1970s, Guzmán's students controlled most of the university, and slowly began a systematic infiltration of the peasant communities.

When I finally met Juan Granda, he was in what was once Guzmán's kitchen. Granda had arrived in Ayacucho in 1970, by which time Guzmán was at the height of his power in the university. Guzmán was responsible for the hiring and firing all those who came to the university. 'This house,' Granda said, 'was the Kremlin. Only very close friends were allowed here. And with Guzmán you were either a close friend or a servant.'

The Guzmán Granda described was different from the one I learned about in Arequipa. The mountains of Ayacucho had changed him. Guzmán, was now wearing a dark suit. There was no smoking in class. There was no interruptions. There was no conversation until ten minutes before the end when there were questions. He never smiled. Like his wife, he never spoke to anyone in the streets. He wore thick-rimmed glasses and saw everything as a battle between Democracy and Authority or Idealism and Materialism. He spoke well, gesticulating, and writing his arguments 'one, two, three, four, five' on the blackboard. He was a schematic thinker.

He did not have an impressive intellect, but it was effective among his students, the poor campesinos, the sons of peons from haciendas, who had come to the modern world of the city. 'He understood their way of life. They didn't have to think. This was how he had got his nickname.'

His nickname?

'Shampoo,' said Juan Granda. 'Because he brain-washed people.'

Juan Granda last saw Guzmán in 1976, when he resigned from the university. By that time, Sendero, dominating the university, had infiltrated the community. They tilled the fields, and several important Senderistas had married into Indian families. When Guzmán resigned from the university in 1976, it was because, by then, Sendero were ready for a revolution.

Huancayo

Sendero have not yet created a 'liberated zone', an identifiable area capable of reproducing itself. They have, however, established an effective presence in sparsely populated areas like the northern jungle region of the Upper Huallaga. I was unable to visit the northern jungles, but I met a man who had, a photographer, Victor Chacón Vargas, who was one of the very few people also to have visited a Sendero base. In 1987, working for the weekly magazine *Caretas*, he was captured twice by Sendero. During our conversation, the lights went out; there had been an attack on the pylons in Huancayo.

Chacón had travelled to Uchiza, a small town 350 miles north of Ayacucho following a report that Sendero had attacked a police station, killing seven policemen, gouging out the eyes and testicles of one officer. He had been in Uchiza a matter of minutes when three Indians appeared, each about twenty years old, wearing jeans with pistols shoved down their belts. They pushed him and several other journalists into a car and drove to the end of the airstrip. Their documents were taken away; they were interrogated one by one; and finally they were moved out of the town, awaiting orders from 'higher up'.

They waited all day, and, when it grew dark, they were led across the river. Chacón said, 'We walked through the jungle and were presented to a man with a Korean machine-gun on his back—it had been taken from one of the policemen. Mosquitoes were everywhere, and he began a political lecture that would go on for two hours: Mao says . . . Mariátegui says . . . President Gonzalo says . . . All jargon. I tried to look as if I was concentrating, but I was thinking of the mosquitoes, my house in Lima, my wife.'

There was no need to be afraid, they were told. If they were spies, they would be killed. If not, not. Sendero had a thousand eyes. A thousand ears.

Chacón was asked why he didn't join the struggle, and he said it was because he was married with two children.

'So am I,' said the Senderista. 'But if I am told to kill my mother, I will kill her. We need people like you. People who know how to speak to the people.'

They spent the night singing revolutionary slogans, and Chacón was released.

And then he was captured again at the end of August, and actually invited to take photographs of the camps.

Chacón's visits were unprecedented. Part of Sendero's success has been attributed to the secrecy of its operations—presupposing a degree of organization and efficiency traditionally so alien to the Peruvian character that President Belaúnde originally concluded that the Sendero could only be foreigners. Even today there are few clear ideas as to how the leadership operates. James Anderson, probably the leading expert on Sendero, describes a rigidly vertical organization in which a 'co-ordination committee' presides over regional committees that preside over regional sub-committees that preside over cells of between five and nine members. Only one member of a cell will have any communication with the layer of leadership above him.

Lima

Sendero's hermetic secrecy derives from the guerrilla campaign of 1965 when everybody seemed to know everything. Hector Bejar was involved in the 1965 campaign. He led the National Liberation Army, one of the two revolutionary movements at the time. He was captured and sent to prison. Today he works as a doctor in Puno and as a lecturer in Lima's San Marcos University. I met him on my return to Lima. He was one of the last people to have seen Abimael Guzmán—in 1979, when they shared a prison cell after a round-up of prominent left-wingers. Their fellow inmates numbered sixty people, all kept in one small room, and included the ten academics from Ayacucho university who are now the main leaders of Sendero, most notably Osman Morote, son of Dr Efraín Morote who hired Guzmán in the sixties.

'We were,' Bejar said, 'sixty people, co-existing in the same small space day and night, but divided into two groups—Guzmán's and mine. Guzmán's regarded me as a member of the opposition—a petit bourgeois defector. For instance, for Guzmán, Cuba, our inspiration, was an example of one of the most advanced bourgeois democracies in Latin America.

'Guzmán was very formal and dogmatic. He disciplined his group in a calm voice, making them study and memorize Mariátegui in the way one might study the Bible. His level was very elementary, very provincial. *Muy Jesuítico.*'

A photograph taken during Guzmán's brief imprisonment shows that the dandy from La Salle had fattened out, his unshaven face weighed down by jowls, his hair still swept back, but without its sheen.

On 3 December 1979, soon after Guzmán's release, it was proposed that the Armed Struggle begin, or in Sendero's inimitable words, it was proposed 'to forge the First Company in Deeds.' The formal decision was made on 17 March 1980. Guzmán appears to have cited a treatise by Washington Irving on Mohammed. He then gathered the members of his group round him and instructed them to read from the first two acts of *Macbeth*. These acts illustrated, it seems, 'how treason is born.' Two months later Sendero entered the sleepy town of Chuschi and Abimael Guzmán disappeared.

There is a wide gap between the Quechua and the Spanish mind. For the Indian, goals do not have to be accomplished in the five-year cycle of a presidential term. For President Gonzalo it does not matter whether his revolution takes five, twenty-five or seventy-five years. It will take place, that's what matters.

But Guzmán was also said to be dying. Of leukaemia, a serious kidney infection, cancer of the lymph glands and Hodgkinson's disease. But few informed people believed Abimael Guzmán to be dead. And if the armed forces had killed him, they would certainly have produced the body.

Perhaps Guzmán was alive but unwell, and had therefore delegated his responsibilities. Perhaps he had left the country, disappeared. In myth, the hero departs for the unknown, and becomes a hero. Guzmán's secret was his invisibility. It didn't matter whether Abimael Guzmán was alive or dead. He had done enough. On reaching the point where the trail vanished, I found myself indifferent. I had looked forward to an encounter with the 'universal genius' who had created Sendero Luminoso. I had argued that if by some chance he was leading a movement that could successfully challenge both Russia and the United States, then his words would be seen as oracle. At the least, I had hoped to resurrect the persona he had left behind. Now I felt thwarted. Perhaps, I found myself reasoning, if one got to the heart of Stalin and Trotsky one would also find a vacant core, a banality. Perhaps people like that are like that, made of straw.

I remained in no doubt that Sendero Luminoso possessed a shaping character, a dominating personality. Yet the character of Abimael Guzmán seemed so insubstantial: the loather of Gershwin, the lover of *Pepito de mi corazón*, the pedestrian thinker, the 'anonymity', a man with whom it was possible to spend seven whole years and remember nothing.

When I returned to Lima, however, I talked to a friend, who had bought the house once owned by Dr Efraín Morote in Ayacucho. 'Speak to Dr Efraín Morote Best,' my friend said. 'He will make you uncomfortable. He will mentally undress you as you sit before him. He will make you laugh simply out of nervous fear. He is filled with brilliant hatred.'

What did he hate? 'Everything,' said my friend. 'Except Chinese cashew nuts and Albanian olive oil.'

I knew little about Dr Efraín Morote Best. I knew that he had been the rector at the university at Ayacucho, the one who had recruited Guzmán. I knew that he was an eminent anthropologist; that at Cuzco University he had been a famous joker and party-goer—an extrovert—until the early 1950s when he suffered a complete change of character. 'He avoided all engagements,' said a colleague. 'He joined the Communist Party and dressed like a Mormon in a lace cravat.' I knew, finally, that one of Morote's sons was imprisoned as a suspected Senderista, that his son Osmán was considered to be one of Sendero's most important leaders.

I discovered more. I learned that General Clemente Noel, the first military commander in Ayacucho, had always believed that Morote was the true leader, 'the high priest of Sendero'.

But Morote did not give interviews, and no one knew where he lived.

I discovered the number of Morote's sister. I rang her, a few days after the security forces had captured Morote's daughter Katia. She was suspected of an arson attack in the Lima suburb of Pueblo Libre.

The sister was polite. And early the next morning I received a call from Morote himself. I was surprised. He spoke an elegant,

191

Castilian Spanish. He agreed to see me, giving an address in Chaclacayo, twenty miles north of Lima.

In Chaclacayo, there was no Lima mist, and the sky was a cloudless blue. I walked up a street named Eucalyptus. Mountain dust covered the lawns and rose bushes. Half-way up on the right was a large yellow house. There was a man kicking a ball. Otherwise no one was about.

Dr Morote came down the steps to greet me, unlocking the gate. He was a small man, in a black cardigan, black trousers and a white shirt open at the neck. His hair was greyer than his moustache and swept back from his face. It was difficult to judge whether he is Spanish or mestizo.

We went up to a room of books, and Morote made idle chat—about the weather in Chaclacayo, how much more pleasant it was than in Lima—and his niece brought me coffee. She then went over to his desk and began fiddling. It was a tape-recorder. I, the interviewer, was being taped. I began sweating, something that had never happened during any other interview I could remember.

I mentioned the increasing European interest in Sendero Luminoso, lamenting the impossibility of finding anyone to speak for the movement. I said that I had been to Ayacucho and that if I had been born a poor *serrano* in those hills, I would be sympathetic to Sendero. I said all this to encourage Morote, but I also meant it.

'Sendero Luminoso is a political party,' Dr Morote said, with a superior smile. 'The Marxist-Leninist-Maoist Communist Party of Peru. Its objectives are to transform the dialectics of Peru, no matter how long this takes.'

I drew a comparison with the architects of Europe's cathedrals, who did not live to see their work complete.

'If you like, politics are today's equivalent to the Church.' But more than anything else it was a very intense battle between two classes. On the one side was the Peruvian Communist Party, and on the other the bourgeois state with its army, its police, its bureaucracy. 'The man who governs Peru and calls himself Pérez—I refer to him by his mother's name because he has a mother's mind—doesn't recognize there's a war on. And it is a war. There is no place for neutrals. Those in the centre will be killed by the cross-fire. It was a historical necessity to take a position, a law of history and a law of nature.' For Morote, García was the last hope of the Peruvian bourgeois democracy. 'But a monkey who dresses in silk remains a monkey.'

He mentioned that there were now only two or three regions in Peru that had not witnessed Sendero activitity. The movement's methods of advance and retreat resembled those of the communists in China, where Morote spent four years working on the Spanish translation of Mao's works. Throughout our conversation, Morote referred to China and its leaders. Later, when I expressed regret that the Peruvian novelist José María Arguedas is not translated more into English, Morote said, as if in answer, that, 'in China there are translations.'

'The China of 1911 is very similar to the present epoch in Peru,' Morote said. 'But then again, this isn't a movement for Peru, this is a movement for the whole of Latin America.'

'What do you see happening in Peru?'

'It will be the same fight, only more intense, more radical, more triumphant.'

'And the violence? How does the Sendero condone that?'

'Violence is part of the human condition. Violence in politics is not only necessary, it is indispensable. We are discussing a new birth, and a new birth is always produced in blood. As in a Caesarian operation, the child insists on living.'

And, by analogy I assumed, the mother might die. The day I met Morote, two officials from García's party were killed in a car bomb, the newspaper reproducing their mangled bodies on the front page. As his niece was preparing coffee, a bus was stopped on the road to Ica in which Sendero discovered two Guardia Civil among the passengers and later shot them in the head outside on the tarmac.

I asked Morote whether he seriously believed that the Peruvian peasant understood a thing about Mao or Mariátegui.

'Life is a permanent contradiction between those who know and those who don't. The people can understand, in their fashion, that the problem of this country is an unfeeling bourgeoisie incapable of changing the situation, either by reason or by force.' The reply, simple and polished, was terrifying. I remembered a sentence from Conrad: 'He would have been a splendid leader of an extreme party.'

I asked about those who were simply indifferent.

'When one has a bottle of whisky, one doesn't drink it all at the same time. One drinks it little by little. The same with indifferent, neutral people. Each day, they will be less indifferent. Each day the badly informed will be less badly informed. It's a question of time. It's part of the philosophy of both China and the Peruvian Indian.'

There was the Sendero patience.

I mentioned Guzmán. Morote smiled. I wondered if I had met the king-maker.

'Guzmán is important but not indispensable. I worked with him for seven years. He was a person of the utmost intelligence, culture and sensitivity. A man who knows as much of Shakespeare as of Cervantes, who understands the music of Liszt as well as the music of Schumann, who began by understanding Marx, Lenin, Stalin.'

I asked if Guzmán was political when Morote first met him, when Guzmán first came to Ayacucho.

'Yes. Because he is *Homo sapiens*.'

But how did he make the change from being a quiet introverted student of philosophy to a terrorist, a proponent of the Armed Struggle?

'The mind is always capable of great leaps. I haven't got Abimael Guzmán's, and I can't know the leaps it took. But it's clear that without the Armed Struggle, the situation wouldn't change.'

'Is Guzmán alive?'

Morote's expression doesn't change. 'When one dies, one lives. Life continues. Marx has been dead many years, but today he is more alive than ever.'

We talked of other things, of Cervantes, Vargas Llosa and Hong Kong, 'a turbulent, congested city'. Morote revealed that he was ill and that he now worked only on a book about the mythologies, legends and religions of Peru. I told him of my experience in Ayacucho, and he brought down from the shelf a folder containing information on the *pistacos* for the last four centuries. It included Cristóval de Molina's reference in 1571:

For in year 1560 and not before, it was held and believed
by the Indians that an ointment from the bodies of the
Indians had been sent for from Spain to cure a disease
for which there was no medicine there.

I asked why the myth had resurfaced now.
 'Because of the killing of campesinos by the armed forces.'
 'Doesn't Sendero kill them too?'
 'Yes, but always in public, and after a people's trial.'
 'What about reports of women who cut men's throats like
chickens?'
 'Absolute propaganda,' he said.
 My mind was full of questions. I asked why Sendero refused to
speak to the government.
 'What for? So they can be destroyed by them? When García
Pérez says he wants a dialogue—that's what *he* wants.'
 And journalists? Why did Sendero never speak to journalists?
 Morote said journalists were killed here. I thought he was
joking. Kill journalists? I said.
 'A journalist is never objective. He takes sides. He is a man
who lives in the present. I live for the future.'
 I felt uneasy. 'Why have you agreed to see me?'
 'My sister said you sounded nice on the phone.'
 There was a silence: *because I sounded nice on the phone?* The
tape continued recording. His niece, sitting behind the desk, stared
at me. There was the sound of a shoe tapping. Morote cleared his
throat and said, 'You haven't finished your coffee.'
 I swallowed. The coffee was cold. I was thinking of Morote,
how he revealed nothing about Sendero and nothing about his
relationship to it, and yet displayed complete familiarity with its
activities.
 I asked one last question.
 'Do you know the words of *Pepito de mi corazón*?'

The author gratefully acknowledges the information and
assistance provided by James Anderson, whose pamphlet 'Sendero
Luminoso: A New Revolutionary Model?' is published by the
Institute for the Study of Terrorism.

IAN HAMILTON
J. D. SALINGER
VERSUS
RANDOM HOUSE,
INC.

J. D. Salinger *versus* Random House, Inc.

Four years ago, I wrote to the novelist J.D. Salinger, telling him that I proposed to write a study of his 'life and work'. Would he be prepared to answer a few questions? I could either visit him at his home in Cornish, New Hampshire, or I could put my really very elementary queries in the mail—which did he prefer? I pointed out to him that the few sketchy 'facts' about his life that had been published were sometimes contradictory and that perhaps the time had come for him to 'set the record straight.' I assured him that I was a serious 'critic and biographer', not at all to be confused with the fans and magazine reporters who had been plaguing him for thirty years. I think I even gave him a couple of dates he could choose from for my visit.

All this was, of course, entirely disingenuous. I knew very well that Salinger had been approached in this manner maybe a hundred times before with no success. The idea of his 'record' being straightened would, I was aware, be thoroughly repugnant to him. He didn't want there to *be* a record, and—so far as I could tell—he was passionate in his contempt for the whole business of 'literary biography'.

I had not, then, expected a response to my approach. On the contrary, I had written just the sort of letter that Salinger—as I imagine him—would heartily despise. At this stage, *not* getting a reply was the essential prologue to my plot. I had it in mind to attempt not a conventional biography—that would have been impossible—but a kind of *Quest for Corvo*, with Salinger as quarry. According to my outline, the rebuffs I experienced would be as much part of the action as the triumphs—indeed, it would not matter much if there *were* no triumphs. The idea—or one of the ideas—was to see what would happen if orthodox biographical procedures were to be applied to a subject who actively set himself to resist and even to forestall them.

And Salinger seemed to be the perfect subject. He was, in any real-life sense, invisible, as good as dead, and yet for many he still held an active mythic force. He was famous for not wanting to be famous. He claimed to loathe any sort of public scrutiny and yet he had made it his practice to scatter just a few misleading clues. It seemed to me that his books had one essential element in common: their author was anxious, over-anxious, to be loved. And, very nearly from the start, he *had* been loved—perhaps more whole-heartedly than any other American writer since the war. *The Catcher in the Rye* exercises a unique seductive power—not just for new young readers who discover it, but for the million or so original admirers like myself who still view Holden Caulfield with a fondness that is weirdly personal, almost possessive.

In gratitude for all this, Salinger's readers have granted him much fame and money and, if he has not altogether turned these down, he has been consistently churlish in accepting them. Now he won't even let us *see* what he is working on. Is he sulking? If so, where did we all go wrong? Or is he teasing us—testing our fidelity and, in the process, making sure that we won't ever totally abandon him? These were the sort of questions my whimsical biographer would play around with.

And so I got him started by firing off about two dozen form-letters to all the Salingers listed in the Manhattan telephone directory: where did the family Salinger come from, I asked, and did any of these Salingers happen to know the novelist J.D.? I was hoping here to tap the well-known American hunger for genealogy and, sure enough, the replies came storming back. But they were neither entertaining nor informative. Nobody knew anything of J.D., except that he had turned into a hermit, and several had never heard of him at all.

But about three weeks later, I got a letter from J.D. Salinger himself. One of *my* letters, it seems, had been received by his sister, and another by his son—both of them listed in the Manhattan phone-book. Salinger berated me for harassing his family 'in the not particularly fair name of scholarship'. He didn't suppose he could stop me writing a book about him, but he thought he ought to let me know—'for whatever little it may be worth'—that he had suffered so many intrusions on his privacy that he could endure no more of it—not 'in a single lifetime'.

The letter was touching, in a way, but also just a shade repellent, too pleased with its own polish for me to accept it as a direct cry from the heart. And yet there could be no mistaking its intent.

According to my original plan (that Salinger might perhaps be lured into the open), it could be said that things were working out quite well. And yet this human contact, icy though it was, did give me pause. Up to now, I'd been dallying with the *idea* of Salinger; he was a fictional character, almost, and certainly a symbolic one in the fable of American Letters. He said he wanted neither fame nor money and he'd contrived to get extra supplies of both—much more of both, in fact, than might have come his way if he'd stayed in the market-place along with everybody else. Surely, I'd been reasoning in my more solemn moments, there was some lesson to be learned from his 'career'. To what extent was Salinger the victim of America's cultural star-system; to what extent its finest flower? American intellectuals look with compassion on those Eastern bloc writers who have been silenced by the State, but here, in their own culture, a greatly loved author had elected to *silence himself.* He had freedom of speech but what he had ended up wanting more than anything else, it seemed, was the freedom to be silent. And the power to silence—to silence anyone who wanted to find out why he had stopped speaking.

And yet, here was this letter, obliging me to face up to the presence of the man himself. He wanted to be left alone.

I wrote back to Salinger, saying that his letter had certainly made me think but that in spite of it I had decided to go ahead with my book. I would undertake, however, to observe some ground rules. Since, until 1965, he had been in the 'public domain' but thereafter had elected not to be, I would not pursue my research beyond that date. I would also undertake not to bother his family and friends. He could still change his mind about seeing me, or about answering some questions, but I didn't suppose he would. My hope was, I said, that if he were eventually to read my book he might soften his view—not just of me, but of what was possible, decently possible, in a genre such as this.

To myself, I issued one or two instructions. I would not attempt to seek out his ex-wife, his children or his sister. I would permit myself to write letters to people who had been friends of his during his writing (or publishing) years, but I would not surprise them on the telephone, nor persist in my letter-writing if two of my letters were to go unanswered. I would make it clear, where I thought there might be any doubt, that Salinger was against what I was doing. And so on. I was trying to make myself sound 'decent'—not just to Salinger, but to myself. On the one hand, I really didn't see why I should extinguish my curiosity about this Salinger phenomenon: I was by no means alone in wanting to know more about him. On the other hand: at what point does decent curiosity become indecent?

And that, more or less, is what I did, completing a manuscript entitled *J.D. Salinger: A Writing Life*, which I delivered to my publishers, Random House, in July, 1985. After a couple of weeks, news came that it had been accepted for publication. A further sum of money was released, and I was advised that the Random House lawyers would need to 'clear' my text before it could be sent to press.

A few weeks later, a legal questionnaire arrived: a routine set of queries to do with possible libels. I was also asked about the quotations from Salinger's letters. I had quoted from these fairly extensively, anxious as I was to communicate my subject's 'tone'. The lawyers wanted to know how much I'd quoted, what proportion of the whole? I did a count and, where I could, I worked out what percentage of each letter had been used. The average—if one viewed the body of available letters as a single 'collection'—was just under twenty-five per cent. Rather to my surprise, the lawyers decided that this amount of borrowing would fall within the limits of 'fair use'. The book was passed for press.

In the fullness of time, proofs arrived, then page proofs, and—in the spring of 1986—bound galleys. Publication was scheduled for the autumn, and it was proposed that the bound sheets, marked 'Please do not quote for publication' should be sent out to possible reviewers. A proof of the cover was prepared, and my photograph was taken up against a wall. And the same kind of thing was happening in England. The lawyers for Heinemann in London had checked out the manuscript and passed it for publication—or at any rate they had not raised any strenuous objections. One formed the impression that they would quite like to see what happened in the States before taking the plunge. Even so, the *Observer* newspaper had bought British serial rights and discussions were begun about which extracts, if any, it might use.

So far, so good. I can't say that I was actually looking forward to publication of the book. It was not, in those days, really the book I had wanted it to be. It was too nervous and respectful, and in many ways disabled by my anxiety to assure Salinger that I was not a rogue. But it was workmanlike; it had far more facts about the man than you could find anywhere else; it had (thanks to the letters) something of his tone of voice, his presence. And in its literary-critical aspects, it had, I thought, some useful things to say about the relationship between the author's life and work. It was *all right*. All the same, I could predict that, if it were to be pushed as a 'biography', there might be some disappointed buyers. Whatever its merits, the book had by no means solved the 'mystery' of Salinger.

To people who asked me about the book, I'd tend to say: 'It isn't much. Don't get the idea that it's a *biography*, because it isn't. But it's not bad.' The one or two pre-publication notices I saw during the early summer of 1986 suggested that this, or something rather like this, would be how most critics would eventually react. Well, so what? At least Salinger couldn't complain that he had been re-glamourized. Indeed, I think I still believed that he might 'rather like' my book. He, more than anyone, would know what I'd left out.

On 25 May 1986, a letter arrived at the offices of Random House from the Manhattan law firm Kaye, Collier and Booze. The same letter, give or take a few formalities, was also delivered to my home in London, and to the offices of Heinemann and the *Observer*. It stated that J.D. Salinger had read bound galleys of my 'biography', that he was displeased by my use of his unpublished letters and that unless these quotations were removed forthwith he would take all necessary legal steps to have the book enjoined.

I was not too worried. It was a disappointment that Salinger didn't like what I had done, but then I had no doubt been a trifle foolish to imagine that he would. As to the legal angle: well, we were presumably on safe ground. After all, had not the Random House lawyers declared my quotations to be 'fair use'? It had never really occurred to me to wonder if they might be wrong. I telephoned them from London, expecting to be reassured that Salinger's mouthpiece was merely 'trying it on' and that he 'didn't stand a chance'.

T he voice at the other end of the line, although controlled and cordial, somehow lacked the airy depth that I'd expected. I wouldn't say it sounded anxious; at the same time, though, it wasn't picking up on my offhand opening remarks. There was a chance, it seemed to be saying, that we might have a Problem. Yes, it was quite true that they, the lawyers, had judged my quotations to fall within the limits of 'fair use'. In the light of Salinger's intervention, however, it might be politic to examine the 'fair use' definition more closely. Also, it might turn out to be a matter for concern that the word-counts I had done were not precisely accurate. I had often failed to include in my counts odd words and phrases from Salinger's letters which I had deployed as links *between* actual quotations. No matter, apparently, that the overall word-count would still work out at around twenty-five per cent. By the end of this exchange, I had begun to sense a slight frosting of the atmosphere.

Soon after, I was summoned urgently to New York—so urgently that my arrival coincided with the beginning of a public holiday. When I eventually made contact with my summoners, it was put to me that I should reduce the amount of direct quotation in the book so as to make it more acceptable to the 'other side'. I spent a week hacking and juggling so that no more than ten words remained from any single letter. The excised quotations I rewrote as reported speech, taking care not to use Salinger's own words— changing 'movie' to 'motion picture', for example. Some of this labour seemed to me ludicrous, but after a while I began to take a certain abstract pride in making my reports fit, exactly, the space taken by the original Salinger quotation. Even so, it was unpleasant work and I disliked having to throw out most of Salinger's best lines. In almost every instance, I was deadening his language; I was making him seem duller than he was. Whose interests did this serve? Salinger's earliest letters are all style, all show. There was never a great deal of factual content. The 'fact' I wanted to communicate was that he wrote letters in the way he did.

This was not, by now, the sort of grumble to be raised at Random House. For a start, there was no one I could raise it with. The editorial department had fallen silent, and the law department had a job to do. In the offices of American publishers, an author can measure his current rating, and perhaps his future prospects, as soon as he steps out of the elevator and presents himself at the front desk. If your stock is high, you will immediately be recognized, your name will have been remembered. More likely than not, you will be kept waiting no more than a few minutes before you are ushered into the almost genial presence of your Editor. As you move through the corridors, between the desks, you will perhaps be greeted with a wave, a nod, an upbeat 'Hi, there' from the Team, of which you might now feel yourself to be an honoured, if honorary, member. I have had one or two such golden moments and I treasure them. If things are going less than well, however—if, alack, there is any sort of Problem with your Project, then you will soon enough be made to know it. The receptionist will have forgotten who you are, and will ask you to spell your name a couple of times before she eventually phones it through. The Team will be polite enough, but strained. Your Editor will be—shall we say?—preoccupied. You will be given the feeling that you (just like your manuscript) have suddenly become provisional, *sub judice*.

My publishers could, I am aware, easily have backed off: they could have withdrawn the book. The news from Britain indicated that the intrepid *Observer* had already cancelled its serialization plans and was demanding reimbursement of all monies paid. I could hardly expect Random House to thank me for having raised some interesting points of law, for sharpening up their thinking on the matter of 'fair use'. Evidently, I was getting a bit touchy. After all, look at what had come to pass. J.D. Salinger, my admired quarry, had finally been forced to speak, and his first words had been: 'It's you I hate. You are a snooper and a thief.'

And it was no good looking to my other half, my old companion-biographer, for reassurance or consolation. He regarded Salinger's letters as a *coup* and was in no mood to equivocate. His job was done.

He would also have been confident that Salinger would not press his lawsuit. Sooner or later, if Salinger did persevere, he would be obliged to make a personal appearance—either in a courtroom or in the offices of the Random House attorneys. He would be required, at the very least, to give a deposition. That's to say, an interview. And, as we knew all too well, this man didn't give interviews. Relax.

Ian Hamilton

By September, the rewriting had been done. There were now only about 200 of Salinger's words left in the manuscript. The revised text was type-set and a second set of galleys was produced. A copy of the 'new book' was despatched to Salinger's lawyers on 18 September. The confident prediction was that they would appreciate our efforts and allow the Project to go forward without further challenge.

This confidence seemed to be well-founded. Although we might have begun to have our fleeting doubts, there surely was in American law a concept of 'fair use'. Indeed, as I now learned, the rule is codified as follows:

> In determining whether the use made of a work in any particular case is a fair use, the factors to be considered shall include:
> 1. The purpose and character of the use, including whether such use is of a commercial nature or is for non-profit educational purposes.
> 2. The nature of the copyrighted work.
> 3. The amount and substantiality of the portion used in relation to the copyrighted work as a whole.
> 4. The effect of the use upon the potential market for or value of the copyrighted work.

On clause one—'the purpose and character of the use'—we would plead that *J.D. Salinger: A Writing Life* was a sober, responsible work of scholarship, that even though we could not (or could we?) describe its purpose as 'non-profit', we could certainly claim it to be educational. On clause three—'the amount used'—we would simply say that from over 30,000 words we had quoted a mere 200. And on clause four—'the effect on the value of the letters'—we would contend that Salinger would never put these letters up for sale, nor publish them himself. In other words, there was no 'potential market . . . value'.

It was with clause two—'the nature of the copyrighted work'—that we envisaged the chief difficulty. After all, these letters were unpublished. Nearly all of the available precedents were concerned with material that had already been in print. 'Unpublished', in Salinger's case, almost certainly meant 'never-to-be-published'.

206

And it was in this respect that the 'Salinger case' (as it was now beginning to be called) differed most strikingly from the case which his lawyers were citing as their precedent: the case of Harper and Row versus the *Nation* magazine. In this dispute, the text in question was some 300 words from an autobiography by Gerald Ford. Harper and Row, the publishers, had sold serial rights in the book to *Time* magazine. Before *Time* was ready to publish its extracts, the *Nation* jumped in with a substantial quotation from Ford's most (perhaps only) newsworthy chapter, the one in which he reveals his feelings about the pardoning of Nixon. *Time* cancelled its serialization contract and Harper and Row sued the *Nation*, eventually securing a Supreme Court judgement in their favour. On the face of it, this judgement had scant bearing on the detail of our Problem: it was a dispute about commerce, about the right to sell. Salinger was defending his right not to sell.

Even so, his lawyers evidently felt that by this ruling the balance of judicial sympathy had been tilted against any 'fair use' line of defence (the line taken by the *Nation*). A week after receiving the new galleys, the 'September galleys' as they were henceforth to be known, Salinger filed suit, asserting that my book still drastically infringed his copyright and that he would be 'irreparably harmed' if publication and distribution were allowed to proceed. On 3 October 1986, a New York District Court granted Salinger a temporary restraining order. This meant simply that the book had to be delayed so that both sides could have a chance to marshal their arguments.

As part of this marshalling, I was required to swear an affidavit. In this, I described my finding of the Salinger letters and my reasons for wanting to include material from them in my book. I had also to describe the damage that would befall me if my book were to be banned: damage not just to the pocket but also to the 'reputation'. And I also had to make it clear that I had gone to some lengths to placate Salinger and avoid any copyright infringement. I claimed, for instance, that I had 'made every effort to avoid quoting the expressive heart of any letter . . . What I attempted to do . . . was to give a true account of events without impinging on Mr Salinger's word-choice and expressive

Ian Hamilton

devices.' This was the first time I had heard, let alone used, the phrase 'expressive heart'.

In New York, Salinger was required to formalize his accusations. In his affidavit, he described himself as an 'author of some renown' who had 'elected, for personal reasons, to leave the public spotlight entirely.' He had shunned all publicity for twenty years and was now a private citizen. On reading my book, he had been 'utterly dismayed' to find that a large part of it—'the core'—was, as he put it, *in my own words*. (The underlining here was one of the very few flickers of authentic Salingerese to appear in his testimony.) He recognized that, in the September galleys, some changes had indeed been made, but these were merely 'cosmetic'. For all my 'inartful' fiddling with word-order and vocabulary, I was still effectively a thief. I had used his literary property to 'flesh out an otherwise lifeless and uninteresting biography.' Although it was true that he had no thoughts of ever publishing these letters, he none the less claimed that they were worth a lot of money, and he didn't see why someone else—someone like me—should pick up any part of it. His 'past literary successes', 'particularly in context with (his) twenty years of public inaccessibility or "silence"', rendered his letters 'most uncommonly valuable literary property'.

All in all, the document made for a depressing read. Salinger, obliged to give an account of himself at last, speaks in a voice that is not even remotely like his own. He would never, in real life, I could have sworn, describe himself as an author of renown, nor boast—as he did here—of the 'bestsellerdom' his books had 'most fortunately' managed to achieve. Now and again a word like 'inartful' or 'cosmetic' did seem as if it might have fallen from his lips, but otherwise, this—his first autobiographical statement for two decades—was written in what one might call 'litilingo', the language of the courts. The whole thing, I was pretty sure, had been drafted by Kaye, Collier and Booze. And when these worthies did try to pep things up, the effect almost always was to demean their client even further—as when they had him say that, if my book were to reach the stores, the injury to Salinger would be 'grave and wholly irreparable' because 'the proverbial cat will be let out of the bag.' The cat? The bag? Could Salinger really have said this, or something like it? Or was this but another irony in this case of many

208

ironies: J.D. Salinger protecting his own words but forced to do so in the words of others? There was a sadness and absurdity in the spectacle of two authors speaking to each other in this strenuously mediocre way.

The case, I soon heard, would come up some time in December. In the meantime, though, there would need to be further low-grade dialogue between the principals: between Salinger and his loathed 'biographer', myself. Each of us was to be interrogated by lawyers from the other side. This was the moment that we, the defendants, had been waiting for and thought would never happen, the moment when poor Salinger would at last be forced to leave his Cornish lair. His affidavit might easily have been prepared by mail or on the telephone; his deposition, though, would have to be 'in person'. He would have to submit to an interview, face to face, with lawyers representing *me*. For myself, I was convinced he wouldn't do it. But he did.

Salinger came to New York on 10 October, 1986, and was interviewed by Robert Callagy of the law firm Satterlee and Stephens (representing Random House and me). Callagy, who has confessed to feeling mildly awed by the prospect of conducting the first extended 'Salinger interview', described his sixty-eight-year-old victim as 'remarkably well-preserved, though somewhat deaf . . . He is greying, with stark features. He is well dressed and appears quite athletic. He comes across more as a business man than as an author.' Salinger was polite and accommodating, but somewhat aristocratic, not to say disdainful, in his manner.

Throughout the actual questioning, Salinger was well protected by his attorney, Marcia Paul. Whenever he showed signs of perhaps wishing to expand one of his answers, Ms Paul would enter an objection, or instruct him to say nothing. Again, the notion of Salinger having to be instructed *not* to speak was somewhat piquant. Salinger's humour, though, could not have been improved by Robert Callagy's unmerciful attachment to correct procedure. Each letter had to be shown to Salinger so that he could acknowledge his authorship, and with each one he was asked to identify its 'expressive heart' and to say how much of this he thought

I had stolen. Since there are nearly one hundred letters in the overall 'collection', this chapter of the deposition took up several hours, with Salinger every so often wondering if there was not some swifter method of proceeding. Surely the letters simply said what they said?

In his letter to me three years earlier, Salinger had asked me not to 'break into the privacy . . . of a person not reasonably suspected of criminal activity.' I was reminded of this plea more than once during my reading of the transcripts of his deposition:

Callagy: Mr Salinger, when was the last time you wrote any work of fiction for publication?

Salinger: I'm not sure exactly.

Callagy: At any time during the past twenty years, have you written a work of fiction for publication?

Salinger: That has been published, you mean?

Callagy: That has been published.

Salinger: No . . .

Callagy: At any time during the past twenty years, have you written any fiction which has not been published?

Salinger: Yes.

Callagy: Could you describe for me what works of fiction you have written which have not been published?

Salinger: It would be very difficult to do . . .

Callagy: Have you written any full-length works of fiction during the past twenty years which have not been published?

Salinger: Could you frame that a different way? What do you mean by a full-length work? You mean ready for publication?

Callagy: As opposed to a short story or a fictional piece or a magazine submission.

Salinger: It's very difficult to answer. I don't write that way. I just start writing fiction and see what happens to it.

Callagy: Maybe an easier way to approach this is, would you tell me what your literary efforts have been in the field of fiction within the last twenty years?

Salinger: Could I tell you or would I tell you? . . . Just a work of fiction. That's all. That's the only description I can really give it . . . It's almost impossible to define. I work with characters, and as they develop, I just go on from there.

Happily, this present-tense line of questioning was not pursued; most of Callagy's questions centred on the Salinger who *had* written works of fiction for publication—the Salinger of the disputed letters. Time and again, Salinger referred to the author of these letters in the third person. When pressed, he would speak of this other J.D. Salinger as 'gauche', 'callow' or 'effusive'. Fifty years on, how could he—at sixty-eight—be expected to know what had gone on in the mind, in the expressive heart, of this 'exuberant' young man, this former self? 'It's very difficult,' he pleaded, 'I wish . . . you could read letters you wrote forty-six years ago. It is very painful reading.' When asked how often the young man wrote to his friends, Salinger replied: 'Apart from too often? I don't know.'

And a similar kind of reply was made by Dorothy Olding, Salinger's agent, when she came to give her deposition. Asked if Salinger had known about the 'secret' meeting she had had with me (to which, when I gave *my* deposition, I understood she had confessed) she said, 'No.' Asked why she had met me, she said that she had wanted to warn me off, to dissuade me from proceeding with the book. A little later on, Callagy asked her again why she had met me, and this time she simply said: 'I wish I knew.' Her attorney reminded her that she had already given a perfectly good answer to this question.

Salinger's application for a preliminary injunction went to court on 5 November 1986. On that day, Judge Pierre Leval delivered a thirty-page judgement in favour of permitting publication of my Septemberized 'biography'. The reasons supporting his judgement read as follows:

Hamilton's use of Salinger's copyrighted material is

minimal and insubstantial; it does not exploit or appropriate the literary value of Salinger's letters; it does not diminish the commercial value of Salinger's letters for future publication; it does not impair Salinger's control over first publication of his copyrighted letters or interfere with his exercise of control over his artistic reputation. The biographical purpose of Hamilton's book and of the adopted passages are quite distinct from the interests protected by Salinger's copyright. Finally, although both Random House and Hamilton no doubt hope to realize profit from the sales of the book, it is a serious, carefully researched biography of an important literary figure (of whom little is known); its publication is of social and educational value.

The judge noted that the 'fair use' doctrine has to consider 'whether such use is of a commercial nature or is for non-profit educational purposes,' and commented that 'in so saying, the statute somewhat unrealistically paints the world into two corners— the venal commercial and the altruistic instructive':

Hamilton's book cannot be dismissed as an act of commercial voyeurism or snooping into a private being's private life for commercial gain. It is a serious, well-researched history of a man who through his own literary accomplishments has become a figure of enormous public interest. This favours a finding of fair use.

From 'our' point of view (my own and that of Random House), the judgement could hardly have been more complete, more firmly spoken. We had won. Letters and telegrams of congratulation began to arrive, newspapers telephoned to ask about my feelings at this hour of triumph, a new publication date was set. *J.D. Salinger: A Writing Life* was now scheduled for spring, 1987. And I was not, according to the law, a snooper and a thief. Thus vindicated, how could I ever have had doubts?

There was, however, one minor blemish in Judge Leval's masterly handling of the case. He had granted the opposition time in which to organize an 'expedited appeal' against his judgement. This, at the time, seemed but a kindly sop to Salinger, whom Leval obviously admired. What would be the point of appealing against a judgement so comprehensive and whole-hearted, a judgement which had declared that 'Salinger has demonstrated no likelihood of success'? It would be costly, it would be fruitless. Swollen by victory, I felt almost protective towards my adversary: O stubborn one, will nobody in his lawyer-entourage protect him from this folly?

Nobody did. On 3 December, Salinger lodged his appeal to the Second Circuit of the United States Court of Appeals. On 29 January 1987, Judges Newman and Miner reversed the Leval judgement and granted the appellant a preliminary injunction. 'SALINGER BIOGRAPHY IS BLOCKED' announced a front-page headline in the *New York Times*. "'We're delighted," said R. Andrew Booze, the attorney for Mr Salinger. "We've told him of the decision, and he is also delighted" . . . A Random House spokesman said after the Appeals Court ruling yesterday, "We are not going to be able to comment until we've had a chance to study the opinion."' I heard of the decision myself in a five-line paragraph in the one English newspaper which reported it. No telegrams from New York. Indeed, no word at all from Random House. No doubt the front desk was already re-unremembering my name.

Eventually, I did manage to get my hands on a copy of the Newman-Miner judgement—twenty-four pages of it. The text lacked Leval's elegant stylistic flourishes and was, I thought, a good deal more philistine in its approach. Undeniably, however, there was a certain bull-headed impressiveness about it. Where Leval had worked from a reluctance to inhibit what he saw as literary scholarship, these two older men worked from a deep faith in private ownership. They were prepared to admit that my book was pure in motive, that it was indeed 'educational', as required by clause one of the 'fair use' definition. But they did not see that this worthiness of purpose entitled me to 'any special consideration'.

On each of the other three 'fair use' clauses, they disagreed with Judge Leval. On clause two—'the nature of the copyrighted work'—they felt that the work's unpublishedness granted it much greater protection than Leval had seemed prepared to offer, coming close to saying that with unpublished material *there can be no 'fair use'*. On clause four—the 'market value' of the letters—they were similarly fierce. Salinger's agent had claimed that a collection of his correspondence would be worth about half a million dollars. Even though Salinger has said that he will never publish the letters, the Appeal Court afforded him 'the right to change his mind', and disagreed with Leval's view that the 'marketability of the letters will be totally unimpaired' by my paraphrasings.

This view, in fact, derived quite fluently from Newman and Miner's most important disagreement with Leval. This was on the matter of clause three—'the amount and substantiality of the portion used in relation to the copyrighted work as a whole'. In Leval's judgement, it was found that the portion used was 'minimal'. The Appeal Court was unimpressed by this, arguing that Leval had been far too lenient, in too many instances seeming to accept that mere changes of vocabulary and word-order were sufficient to deprive Salinger of copyright protection.

Newman and Miner also believed that Leval had been over-ready to contend that certain words and phrases in Salinger's letters were too 'ordinary' to warrant copyright protection: they were clichés, or common turns of speech, Leval had argued, and could not therefore be thought of as the property of any single author. According to Newman and Miner, though, 'in almost all of those instances where the quoted or paraphrased passages from Salinger's letters contain an "ordinary" phrase, the passage as a whole displays a sufficient degree of creativity as to sequence of thoughts, choice of words, emphasis and arrangement to satisfy the minimum threshold of required creativity. And in all of the instances where that minimum threshold is met, the Hamilton paraphrasing tracks the original so closely as to constitute infringement.' In other words (and how differently *that* phrase now falls upon the ear), I had been wasting my time changing 'movie' to 'motion picture', 'rat' to 'rodent', 'applauding madly' to 'clapping her hands in appreciation', and so on. That elusive, yet-to-be-defined 'expressive heart' was indeed a suffusing sort of essence, untransplantable. The Appeal Court judges summarized as follows:

> To deny a biographer like Hamilton the opportunity to copy the expressive content of unpublished letters is not, as appellees contend, to interfere in any significant way with the process of enhancing public knowledge of history or contemporary events. The facts may be reported. Salinger's letters contain a number of facts that students of his life and writings will no doubt find of interest, and Hamilton is entirely free to fashion a biography that reports these facts. But Salinger has a right to protect the expressive content of his unpublished writings for the term of his copyright, and that right prevails over a claim of fair use . . . Public awareness of the expressive content of the letters will have to await either Salinger's decision to publish or the expiration of his copyright.

In fact, public awareness of the 'expressive content' of Salinger's unpublished letters was instantly extended on the day after this judgement was released. The *New York Times* felt itself free to quote substantially not from my paraphrases but from the Salinger originals which I had so painstakingly and, it now seemed, needlessly attempted not to steal. And the same thing has happened since in several other newspapers and magazines. Simply leafing through the ones I happen to have on my desk this morning, I have counted no fewer than 500 copyrighted words from Salinger's unpublished writings—in papers ranging from the *Times Literary Supplement* to *New York* magazine. Injunctions, of course, can only work if you know in advance that there is a plan to publish. I don't expect that Salinger will sue these journals retrospectively. If he doesn't, can we assume that these 500 words have been released into the public domain, that they are no longer 'unpublished'? Would Newman and Miner now let me *put them back* into my book?

In the legal community, there was a flurry of excitement. This new ruling had raised all sorts of juicy possibilities. 'Fair use' had taken a bad knock. So too had 'paraphrase'. Copyright law might never be the same again. Although none of the outside legal opinions canvassed by the press came down at all firmly on one side or the other, the general feeling seemed to be that here was an important, if not crucial, clash 'between the right to privacy and the right to know'. The Newman-Miner verdict had brought the Copyright Act into direct collision with the First Amendment.

Meanwhile, Salinger was getting more feature-length attention in the press than would surely have resulted from the unimpeded publication of my 'writing life'. After all, was there not a rich new fund of Salinger information to be tapped? For a start, there was my book, which by now the whole of New York seemed to have a copy of, in photostat. Also, for a fee of ten dollars, anyone could drop into the Copyright Office in Washington and consult the full collection of 'unpublished letters'—chronologically arranged and neatly packaged. In order to bring his legal action, Salinger had had to copyright each letter individually, thus making them accessible at a price well below what Random House would have been asking for my book. With all this new data, *New York* magazine ran a seven-page story called 'The Salinger File', and *Newsday* published a pull-out supplement. As *New York* opined: 'In the course of this well-documented lawsuit, the public is learning more about Salinger than it has at any time during the last thirty-four years. And if the precedent-setting case is finally decided in favour of Salinger, the elusive author's influence on future biography, journalism and non-fiction could prove as indelible as his mark on modern fiction.' To date, over one hundred newspaper and magazine articles on Salinger have appeared since he filed suit.

In one of these, Robert Callagy is quoted as saying: 'If you take this opinion (the Appeals Court judgement) to an extreme, what it says is that you can't quote anything that has not been published before, and if you attempt to paraphrase you are at serious peril. Copyright law was created to protect an author in a property right, not to obliterate the past.' Random House, it transpired, had decided to go to the Supreme Court.

In September 1987, Random House applied to the Supreme Court for a 'writ of Certiorari'. There was no guarantee that the Court would agree to ponder it, since out of 3,000 cases offered to them each year, the nine Justices accept about 400.

The Random House petition described in detail the background to the case, and it mounted a spirited attack on the Appeals Court verdict, claiming that it imperilled the writing of all biography, but most particularly the writing of literary biography. By their nature, literary biographies 'are histories of the thoughts and ideas of writers, works on the process of imagination of writers. Such works would often be nearly pointless, not to say superficial, if biographers were not permitted to make some fair, if modest, reference to the full range of published and unpublished writings that illuminated the creative process.' Biographers, it went on to say, were now placed in a 'double bind': their job required them to hunt down 'primary sources', 'to gather information from sources as yet untouched'. But what was the point of such diligence if 'they are not at liberty to quote or convey any of the richness of those materials without facing the risk—perhaps the likelihood—of an injunction'? The Court of Appeals 'had little or no sympathy for the biographer faced with this dilemma.' The Random House petition pointed out that 'in every previous instance in which a plaintiff has attempted to invoke the copyright laws to prevent the appearance of unauthorized biography or history,' the courts had ultimately sided with the sued and that now 'for what may well be the first time in the history of American scholarship, an appellate court has countenanced the effort of a public figure to veto publication of a book of which he disapproves.'

So, history was on our side: legal history, that is to say. The application's rhetoric was plangent and persuasive, and was even buttressed with a tag from Thomas Jefferson about letters being the diary of a man's soul. Waiting for the outcome, some two years after having handed the book in to Random House, I asked myself from time to time: Why don't I feel more victimized, why do I tend to shift my gaze, as Holden Caulfield did, when people yell at me: 'Good luck!'? Maybe it's because, when I really ask myself how this whole thing began, I have to confess that there was more to it than mere literary whimsy. There was more to it than mere 'scholarship'. Although it will seem ludicrous, perhaps, to hear me say so now, I think the sharpest spur was an infatuation, an infatuation which bowled me over at the age of seventeen and which it seems I'd never properly outgrown. Well, I've outgrown it now. The book I fell in love with has broken free of its magician author. But even so I can't rejoice that, whatever happens, my name and J.D. Salinger's will be forever linked as litigants, as foes—in the law school textbooks, on the shelves of the Supreme Court, and in the minds of everyone who reads this, the 'legal' version of my book.

T. CORAGHESSAN
BOYLE
THE MIRACLE AT
BALLINSPITTLE

There they are, the holybugs, widows in their weeds and fat-ankled mothers with palsied children, all lined up before the snotgreen likeness of the Virgin, and McGahee and McCarey among them. This statue, alone among all the myriad three-foot-high snotgreen likenesses of the Virgin cast in plaster by Finbarr Finnegan & Sons, Cork City, was seen one grim March afternoon some years back to move its limbs ever so slightly, as if seized suddenly by the need of a good sinew-cracking stretch. Nuala Nolan, a young girl in the throes of Lenten abnegation, was the only one to witness the movement—a gentle beckoning of the statue's out-thrust hand—after a fifteen-day vigil during which she took nothing into her body but Marmite and soda water. Ever since, the place has been packed with tourists.

Even now, in the crowd of humble countrymen in shit-smeared boots and knit skull-caps, McGahee can detect a certain number of Teutonic or Manhattanite faces above cable-knit sweaters and pendent cameras. Drunk and in debt, on the run from a bad marriage, two DWI convictions and the wheezy expiring gasps of his moribund mother, McGahee pays them no heed. His powers of concentration run deep. He is forty years old, as lithe as a boxer though he's done no hard physical labour since he took a construction job between semesters at college twenty years back, and he has the watery eyes and doleful, dog-like expression of the saint. Twelve hours ago he was in New York, at Paddy Flynn's, pouring out his heart and enumerating his woes for McCarey, when McCarey said, 'Fuck it, let's go to Ireland.' And now here he is at Ballinspittle, wearing the rumpled Levi's and Taiwanese sports coat he'd pulled on in his apartment yesterday morning, three hours off the plane from Kennedy and flush with warmth from the venerable Irish distillates washing through his veins.

McCarey—plump, stately McCarey—stands beside him, bleary-eyed and impatient, disdainfully scanning the crowd. Heads are bowed. Infants snuffle. From somewhere in the distance comes the bleat of a lamb and the mechanical call of the cuckoo. McGahee checks his watch: they've been here seven minutes already and nothing's happened. His mind begins to wander. He's thinking about orthodontics—thinking an orthodontist could make a fortune in this country—when he looks up and spots her, Nuala Nolan, a scarecrow of a girl, an anorectic, bones-in-a-sack sort of girl, kneeling in front of the queue and reciting the Mysteries in a voice parched for food and drink. Since the statue moved she has stuck to her diet of Marmite and soda water until the very synapses of her brain have become encrusted with salt and she raves like a mariner lost at sea. McGahee regards her with awe. A light rain has begun to fall.

And then suddenly, before he knows what's come over him, McGahee goes limp. He feels light-headed, transported, feels himself sinking into another realm, as helpless and cut adrift as when Dr Beibelman put him under for his gall-bladder operation. He breaks out in a sweat. His vision goes dim. The murmur of the crowd, the call of the cuckoo and the bleat of the lamb all meld into a single sound—a voice—and that voice, ubiquitous, timeless, all-embracing, permeates his every cell and fibre. It seems to speak through him, through the broad-beamed old hag beside him, through McCarey, Nuala Nolan, the stones and birds and fishes of the sea. 'Davey,' the voice calls in the sweetest tones he's ever heard, 'Davey McGahee, come to me, come to my embrace.'

As one, the crowd parts, a hundred stupefied faces turned towards him, and there she is, the Virgin, snotgreen no longer but radiant with the aquamarine of actuality, her eyes glowing, arms beckoning. McGahee casts a quick glance around him. McCarey looks as if he's been punched in the gut, Nuala Nolan's skeletal face is clenched with hate and jealousy, the humble countrymen and farmwives stare numbly from him to the statue and back again . . . and then, as if in response to a subconscious signal, they drop to their knees in a human wave so that only he, Davey McGahee, remains standing. 'Come to me,' the figure implores, and slowly, as if his feet were encased in cement, his head reeling and his stomach sour, he begins to move forward, his own arms outstretched in ecstasy.

The words of his catechism, forgotten these thirty years, echo in his head: 'Mother Mary, Mother of God, pray for us sinners now and at the hour of our—'

'Yesssss!' the statue suddenly shrieks, the upturned palm curled into a fist, a fist like a weapon, 'and you think it's as easy as that, do you?'

McGahee stops cold, hovering over the tiny effigy like a giant, a troglodyte, a naked barbarian. Three feet high, grotesque, shaking its fist up at him, the thing changes before his eyes. Gone is the beatific smile, gone the grace of the eyes and the faintly mad and indulgent look of the transported saint. The face is a gargoyle's, a shrew's, and the voice, sharpening, probing like a dental tool, suddenly bears an uncanny resemblance to his ex-wife's. 'Sinner!' the gargoyle hisses, 'fall on your knees!'

The crowd gasps. McGahee, his bowels turned to ice, pitches forward into the turf. 'No, no, no!' he cries, clutching at the grass and squeezing his eyes shut. 'Hush,' a new voice whispers in his ear, 'look. You must look.' There's a hand on his neck, bony and cold. He winks open an eye. The statue is gone and Nuala Nolan leans over him, her hair gone in patches, the death's head of her face and suffering eyes, her breath like the loam of the grave. 'Look, up there,' she whispers.

High above them, receding into the heavens like a kite loosed from the string, is the statue. Its voice comes to him faint and distant—'Behold . . . now . . . your sins . . . and excesses'—and then it dwindles away like a fading echo.

Suddenly, behind the naked pedestal, a bright, sunlit vista appears, grape-vines marshalled in rows, fields of barley, corn and hops, and then, falling from the sky with thunderous crashes, a succession of vats, kegs, hogsheads and buckets piling up in the foreground as if on some phantom pier piled high with freight. *Boom, boom, ka-boom, boom,* down they come till the vista is obscured and the kegs mount to the tops of the trees. McGahee pushes himself up to his knees and looks around him. The crowd is regarding him steadily, jaws set, the inclemency of the hanging judge sunk into their eyes. McCarey, kneeling too now and looking as if he's just lurched up out of a drunken snooze to find himself on a subway car on another planet, has gone steely-eyed with the rest of them. And Nuala Nolan, poised over him, grins till the long, naked roots of her teeth gleam beneath the skirts of her rotten gums.

'Your drinking!' shrieks a voice from the back of the throng, his wife's voice, and there she is, Fredda, barefoot and in a snotgreen robe and hood, wafting her way through the crowd and pointing her long, accusatory finger at his poor, miserable, shrinking self. 'Every drop,' she booms and the vasty array of vats and kegs and tumblers swivels to reveal the signs hung from their sweating slats—GIN, BOURBON, BEER, WHISKEY, SCHNAPPS, PERNOD—and the crowd lets out a long exhalation of shock and lament.

The keg of gin. Tall it is and huge, its contents vaguely sloshing. You could throw cars into it, buses, tractor-trailers. But no, never, he couldn't have drunk that much gin, no man could. And beside it the beer, frothy and bubbling, a cauldron the size of a rest home. 'No!' he cries in protest. 'I don't even like the taste of the stuff.'

'Yes, yes, yes,' chants a voice beside him. The statue is back, Fredda gone. It speaks in a voice he recognizes, though the wheezy, rheumy deathbed rasp of it has been wiped clean. 'Ma?' he says, turning to the thing.

Three feet tall, slick as a seal, the robes flowing like the sea, the effigy looks up at him out of his mother's face drawn in miniature. 'I warned you,' the voice leaps out at him, high and querulous, 'out behind the 7-Eleven with Ricky Reitbauer and that criminal Tommy Capistrano, cheap wine and all the rest.'

'But Mom, *Pernod?*' He peers into the little pot of it, a pot so small you couldn't boil a good Safeway chicken in it. There it is. Pernod. Milky and unclean. It turns his stomach even to look at it.

'Your liver, son,' the statue murmurs with a resignation that brings tears to his eyes, 'just look at it.'

He feels a prick in his side and there it is, his liver—a poor piece of cheesy meat, stippled and striped and purple—dangling from the plaster fingers. 'God,' he moans, 'God Almighty.'

'Rotten as your soul,' the statue says.

McGahee, still on his knees, begins to blubber. Meaningless slips of apology issue from his lips as from the great maw of the fortune cookie machine—'I didn't mean . . . it wasn't . . . how could I know?'—when all of a sudden the statue shouts, 'Drugs!' with a voice of iron.

Immediately the scene changes. The vats are gone, replaced with bales of marijuana, jars of pills in every colour imaginable, big, overbrimming tureens of white powder, a drugstore display of airplane glue. In the background, running in a mad frazzled skein to the distant horizon, are bedraggled Turks, grinning Laotians,

Peruvian peasants with hundreds of scrawny children propped like puppets on their shoulders.

'But, but—' McGahee stutters, rising to his feet to protest, but the statue doesn't give him a chance, won't, can't, and the stentorian voice—his wife's, his mother's, no one's and everyone's, he even detects a trace of his high school principal's in there—the stentorian voice booms: 'Sins of the Flesh!'

He blinks his eyes and the Turks and their bales are gone. The backdrop now is foggy and obscure, dim as the mists of memory. The statue is silent. Gradually the poor sinner becomes aware of a salacious murmur, an undercurrent of moaning and panting and the lubricious thwack and whap of the act itself. 'Davey,' a girl's voice calls, tender, pubescent, 'I'm scared.' And then his own voice, bland and reassuring: 'I won't stick it in, Cindy, I won't, I swear . . . or maybe, maybe just . . . just an inch . . .'

The mist lifts and there they are, in teddies and negligées, in garter-belts and sweat-socks, naked and wet and kneading their breasts like dough. 'Davey,' they moan, 'oh, Davey, fuck me, fuck me, fuck me,' and he knows them all, from Cindy Lou Harris and Betsy Butler in the twelfth grade to Fredda in her youth and the sad and ugly faces of his one-night stands and chance encounters, right on up to the bug-eyed woman with the doleful breasts he'd diddled in the rest-room on the way out from Kennedy. And worse. Behind them, milling around in a mob that stretches to the horizon, are all the women and girls he'd ever lusted after, even for a second, the twitching behinds and airy bosoms he'd stopped to admire on the street, the legs he'd wanted to stroke and lips to press to his own. McCarey's wife Beatrice is there and Fred Dolby's thirteen-year-old daughter, the woman with the freckled bosom who used to sunbathe in the tiger-skin bikini next door when they lived in Irvington, the girl from the typing pool and the outrageous little shaven-headed vixen from Domino's Pizza. And as if that weren't enough, there's the crowd from books and films too, Linda Lovelace, Sophia Loren, Emma Bovary, the Sabine women and Lot's wife, even Virginia Woolf with her puckered foxy face and the eyes that seem to beg for a good slap on the bottom. It's too much— all of them murmuring his name like a crazed chorus of Molly Blooms, and yes, she's there too—and the mob behind him hissing, hissing.

He glances at the statue. The plaster lip curls in disgust, the adamantine hand rises and falls and the women vanish. 'Gluttony!' howls the Virgin and all at once he's surrounded by forlornly mooing herds of cattle, sad-eyed pigs and sheep, funeral geese and clucking ducks, a spill of scuttling crabs and claw-waving lobsters, even the odd dog or two he'd inadvertently wolfed down in Tijuana burritos and Cantonese stir-fry. And the scales—scales the size of the Washington Monument—sunk under pyramids of ketchup, peanut butter, tortilla chips, truckloads of potatoes, onions, avocados, peppermint candies and after-dinner mints, half-eaten burgers and fork-scattered peas, the whole slithering wasteful cornucopia of his secret and public devouring. 'Moooooo,' accuse the cows. 'Stinker!' 'Pig!' 'Glutton!' cry voices from the crowd.

Prostrate now, the cattle hanging over him, letting loose with their streams of urine and clots of dung, McGahee shoves his hands into his eyes and cries out for mercy. But there is no mercy. The statue, wicked and glittering, its tiny twisted features clenching and unclenching like the balls of its fists, announces one after another the unremitting parade of his sins: 'Insults of Humanity, False Idols, Sloth, Unclean Thoughts, The Kicking of Dogs and Cheating at Cards!'

His head reels. He won't look. The voices cry out in hurt and laceration and he feels the very ground give way beneath him. The rest, mercifully, is a blank.

When he comes to, muttering in protest—'False idols, I mean like an autographed picture of Mickey Mantle, for Christ's sake?'—he finds himself in a cramped mud-and-wattle hut that reeks of goat dung and incense. By the flickering glow of a bank of votary candles, he can make out the bowed and patchy head of Nuala Nolan. Outside it is dark and the rain drives down with a hiss. For a long moment, McGahee lies there, studying the fleshless form of the girl, her bones sharp and sepulchral in the quavering light. He feels used up, burned out, feels as if he's been cored like an apple. His head screams. His throat is dry. His bladder is bursting.

He pushes himself up and the bony demi-saint levels her

225

tranced gaze on him. 'Hush,' she says, and the memory of all that's happened washes over him like a typhoon.

'How long have I—?'

'Two days.' Her voice is a reverent whisper, the murmur of the acolyte, the apostle. 'They say the Pope himself is on the way.'

'The Pope?' McGahee feels a long shiver run through him.

Nods the balding death's head. The voice is dry as husks, wheezy, but a girl's voice all the same, and an enthusiast's. 'They say it's the greatest vision vouchsafed to man since the time of Christ. Two hundred and fifteen people witnessed it, every glorious moment, from the cask of gin to the furtive masturbation to the ace up the sleeve.' She's leaning over him now, inching forward on all fours, her breath like chopped meat gone bad in the refrigerator; he can see, through the tattered shirt, where her breasts used to be. 'Look,' she whispers, gesturing towards the hunched low entranceway.

He looks and the sudden light dazzles him. Blinking in wonder, he creeps to the crude doorway and peers out. Immediately a murmur goes up from the crowd—hundreds upon hundreds of them gathered in the rain on their knees—and an explosion of flash cameras blinds him. Beyond the crowd he can make out a police cordon, vans and video cameras, CBS, BBC, KDOG and NPR, a face above a trenchcoat that could only belong to Dan Rather himself. 'Holy of holies!' cries a voice from the front of the mob—he knows that voice—and the crowd takes it up in a chant that breaks off into the Lord's Prayer. Stupefied, he wriggles out of the hut and stands, bathed in light. It's McCarey there before him, reaching out with a hundred others to embrace his ankles, kiss his feet, tear with trembling, devoted fingers at his Levi's and Taiwanese tweed— Michael McCarey, adulterer, gambler, drunk and atheist, cheater of the IRS and bane of the Major Deegan—hunkered down in the rain like a holy supplicant. And there, not thirty feet away, is the statue, lit like Betelgeuse and as inanimate and snotgreen as a stone of the sea.

Rain pelts McGahee's bare head and the chill seizes him like a claw jerking hard and sudden at the ruined ancient priest-ridden superstitious root of him. The flash bulbs pop in his face, a murmur of Latin assaults his ears, Sister Mary Magdalen's unyielding face rises before him out of the dim mists of eighth-grade math . . . and then the sudden, imperious call of nature blinds him to all wonder, and he staggers round back of the hut to relieve himself of his two days' accumulation of salts and uric acid and dregs of whiskey. Stumbling, fumbling for his zipper, the twin pains in his groin like arrows driven through him, he jerks out his poor pud and lets fly.

'Piss!' roars a voice behind him, and he swivels his head in fright, helpless before the stream that issues from him like a torrent. The crowd falls prostrate in the mud, cameras whirr, voices cry out. It is the statue, of course, livid, jerking its limbs and racking its body like the image of the Führer in his maddest denunciation. 'Piss on sacred ground, will you?' rage the plaster lips in the voice of his own father, that mild and pacifistic man, 'you unholy insect, you whited sepulchre, you speck of dust in the eye of your Lord and Maker!'

What can he do? He clutches himself, flooding the ground, dissolving the hut, befouling the bony scrag of the anchorite herself.

'Unregenerate!' shrieks the Virgin. 'Unrepentant! Sinner to the core!'

And then it comes.

The skies part, the rain turns to popcorn, marshmallows, English muffins, the light of seven suns scorches down on that humble crowd gathered on the sward, and all the visions of that first terrible day crash over them in hellish simulcast. The great vats of beer and gin and whiskey fall to pieces and the sea of booze floats them, the cattle bellowing and kicking, sheep bleating and dogs barking, despoiled girls and hardened women clutching for the shoulders of the panicked communicants as for sticks of wood awash in the sea, Sophia Loren herself and Virginia Woolf, Fredda, Cindy Lou Harris and McCarey's wife swept by in a blur, the TV vans overturned, the trenchcoat torn from Dan Rather's back and the Gardai sent sprawling—'Thank God he didn't eat rattlesnake,' someone cries—and then it's over. Night returns. Rain falls. The booze sinks softly into the earth, food lies rotting in clumps. A drumbeat of hooves thunders off into the dark while fish wriggle and escargots creep, and Fredda, McCarey, the shaven-headed pizza vixen and all the gap-toothed countrymen and farm-wives and palsied children pick themselves up from the ground amid the curses of the men cheated at cards, the lament of the fallen women and the mad frenzied chorus of prayer that speaks over it all in the tongue of terror and astonishment.

But oh, sad wonder, McGahee is gone.

Today the site remains as it was that night, fenced off from the merely curious, combed over inch by inch by priests and parapsychologists, blessed by the Pope, a shrine as reverenced as Lourdes and the Holy See itself. The cattle were sold off at auction after intensive study proved them ordinary enough, though brands were traced to Montana, Texas and the Swiss Alps, and the food—burgers and snow-cones, rib roasts, fig newtons, extra dill pickles and all the rest—was left where it fell, to feed the birds and fertilize the soil. The odd rib or T-bone, picked clean and bleached by the elements, still lies there on the ground in mute testimony to those three days of tumult. Fredda McGahee Meyerowitz, Herb Bucknell and others cheated at cards, the girl from the pizza parlour and the rest were sent home via Aer Lingus, compliments of the Irish government. What became of Virginia Woolf, dead forty years prior to these events, is not not known, nor the fate of Emma Bovary either, though one need only refer to Flaubert for the best clue to this mystery. And of course, there are the tourism figures—up a whopping 672 per cent since the miracle.

McCarey has joined an order of Franciscan monks and Nuala Nolan, piqued no doubt by her supporting role in the unfolding of the miracle, has taken a job in a pastry shop, where she eats by day and prays for forgiveness by night. As for Davey McGahee himself, the prime mover and motivator of all these enduring mysteries, here the lenses of history and of myth and miracology grow obscure. Some say he descended into a black hole of the earth, others that he evaporated, while still others insist that he ascended to heaven in a blaze of light, Saint of the Common Sinner.

For who hasn't lusted after woman or man or drunk his booze and laid to rest whole herds to feed his greedy gullet? Who hasn't watched them starve by the roadside in the hollows and waste places of the world and who among us hasn't scoffed at the credulous and ignored the miracle we see outside the window every day of our lives? Ask not for whom the bell tolls—unless perhaps you take the flight to Cork City, and the bus or rented Nissan out to Ballinspittle by the Sea, and gaze on the half-size snotgreen statue of the Virgin, mute and unmoving all these many years.

228

CHARLES NICHOLL
A COCK FIGHT

I t was the night before Beauregard's big fight, time for his final preparations. Jo said I could come and watch but—he laid a black, sea-scoured finger to his lips—'no fool questions.' We left the lights of Vauclin and walked inland. The music from the Saturday night *baldoudou* faded. Jo began to sing. He would croon a few lines in his impenetrable Creole, and then it would be the turn of Georges and me to come in with the refrain:

> *Beauregard, Beauregard, Beauregay,*
> *Li bougé comme cou z'éclay . . .*

Beauregard himself was silent. He sat in state in a small cane-stem cage covered with a red cloth. Jo carried the cage with great care, despite all the rum he'd drunk.

Beauregard was a five-year-old fighting cock. This is a good age for a fighter: age was now part of his prowess. He was a *zinga*—a speckled grey—of Venezuelan extraction. Here in Martinique the cocks of Latin America are highly prized. They are nimble and cunning, *très méchant*. They are real *coq gime*—the Creolization of 'game cock'—as opposed to the barnyard mongrels that form the staple of West Indian cocking. Beauregard weighed in at about three pounds and, according to the song we sang, moved like a flash of lightning. He was the pride of Georges, his owner, and of Jo, who was the skipper of Georges's two boats and Beauregard's handler and trainer.

The season had recently begun. It runs from December to May, roughly the length of the dry season. Beauregard had cruised a couple of outings against local opposition, but tomorrow was the big one. This time it wasn't just Georges's money and Jo's esteem that were riding on him, but the prestige of the entire village. Tomorrow, at the cockpit on the edge of Vauclin, Beauregard would meet Tonton, the pride of Trois Ilets across the other side of the island. Rivalry was intense, and the pre-fight betting—not so much on the outcome, for everyone in Vauclin believed that Beauregard would take it, but on such niceties as the duration of the bout and the mode of the *coup de grâce*—had been going on all week.

So too had Beauregard's training. Three times a day he was brought to a shady corner of the yard to spar with another of

Georges's roosters. For sparring he wore a protective hood and leggings, made of sized sackcloth. Placing the hood on him, Jo called him *ti-moine*, little monk. After the spar Beauregard was put in a box in the corner of his pen and covered with straw to sweat. His pen was roomy and shaded by spreading catalpa trees. None of the other roosters lived in such style. He had four separate perches in the pen—a little bit of variety to lessen his *ennui*, for now that he was in training he was brought no hens to tread and was kept away from the daily business of the farmyard. The perches were carefully measured, each the length of the handle of Jo's machete. This encouraged the cock to perch with his feet close together. The cock that is *étroit* (narrow) strikes deadliest.

In a corner of the pen was a square of sand. Here Beauregard fed, so as not blunt his beak on the packed earth of the yard. His day to day diet was cornseed and manioc meal, baked into small loaves. To this, various sharpeners were added, more and more as the fight neared. Eggs were beaten in, butter and molasses, zests of rum. He had hog-plum juice and bitter aloes to purge him, oleander leaf to harden his skin and a herb called *zo-poisson* (fish bone) for general good luck. And he had urine, poured from a little bottle into the mash. *Pipi ti-fi,* Jo was careful to specify. Little girl's pee.

That afternoon, a close clipping from Jo. His neck-hackle was cut back, leaving just a stumpy tonsure of black feathers around the crown, and a furrow of exposed pink skin down the neck and along the back. The purpose of this is to deny the opponent beak-hold: on some islands in the West Indies clipping the neck-hackle is disallowed. He also had his wings clipped a couple of inches, so he didn't fly up too high when striking. The spines of the wing-feathers were then sharpened with a knife, adding another weapon.

And now, the night before the fight, with the moon high and nearing the full, came the final preparation: we were taking him to Auguste.

We left the road. We walked along tracks, past banana groves and plots of cane and isolated farmhouses where dogs set up a racket. We were in a valley called the Coulée d'Or. The plumed tassels of the sugar cane waved gently, though I could feel no breeze. The air seemed still and heavy now we had left the sea.

Jo said the sugar harvest would soon begin. He had worked as a cutter on the neighbouring island of St Lucia, which was why he spoke some English, which was why he had befriended me, which was why I was here right now. We had a casual deal. Jo promised to 'show me life' in Vauclin; I paid for things along the way. Often this meant standing him rounds of rum at one of the waterfront bars, till his lean black face shone, and his peeling old topi slid down over his forehead, and he told me of the wife he had left in San Fernando, Trinidad, and of his daughter called Fête because she was born on Quatorze Juillet, and of the two children he had 'put in the ground', and then the talk would turn to Deborah, an American girl who had passed this way, and Jo would tell me once again that he had 'fucked Deborah no problem,' and at last it would be time to head unsteadily back, me to my room at the town's only hotel, the Auberge les Alizes, Jo to his wood and tin hut in the shanty streets of Pointe Athanase on the edge of Vauclin.

But it meant good things as well. He took me out fishing for snapper and kingfish in *Tranquillité*, a twenty-foot dug-out with an outboard on the back. He cooked me sea-urchin stew. And he taught me the rudiments of Martiniquais Creole, a patchwork chassis of French, Spanish, English and Carib, powered along at breakneck speed by a stripped-down version of French syntax. One of the first Creolisms I learned was *bai-moin un ti-bagay*, 'give me a little something.' Tonight at the *baldoudou* Jo had been through many little somethings, on account of liquor and stakes at the dice stalls. The invitation to accompany him to Auguste's was something in return.

Auguste was what they call a *doctor feuille*, a 'leaf doctor'. The leaf doctor is a healer and minor shaman, a looker into the secrets of herbs and roots, a brewer of *quimbois* or magic potions. Auguste was one of several around Vauclin. When Jo first spoke of him earlier that evening he called him a *tonton macoute*. I was alarmed, thinking of Papa Doc's secret police in Haiti, but it turned out that the term, which literally means 'uncle satchel', originally referred to itinerant herbalists like Auguste.

We were taking Beauregard to Auguste to be blessed and coated with magic *quimbois*. Jo said this would assure his invincibility in the pit tomorrow against Tonton of Trois Ilets. Georges was less convinced. He was of a different generation and class from Jo. At twenty-five he was half Jo's age. His father was, according to Jo, the richest man in Vauclin. There was Indian blood in the family, trading blood. Georges owned farmland, a brick-built house, two boats and a beach buggy. He was educated. He spoke good French. He talked of underdevelopment and the third world and post-colonialism. He laughed at these old superstitions and *quimboiseries*. 'It is the religion of slaves,' he said. But he came along just the same, out of politeness to Auguste, and to keep a close eye on his rooster's welfare.

Jo believed in it all. We were simply doing things *selon les lois*, according to the laws.

The path began to climb through woodland. The volcanic bulk of Mount Vauclin loomed above us in the moonlight. Auguste lived in the foothills, where the flora was more various than down near the sea. After an hour we arrived. A clearing gave onto a farmyard: low buildings, acacia-wood fencing, dogs, pigs, chickens. A group of blacks played dominoes beneath a hurricane lamp. We heard the slap of the dominoes and the calling of the numbers as we came round the last bend.

There were brief greetings, but we kept on walking, round the back of the buildings to a lean-to shed built of wood and palm-thatch. There was candle-light inside, and voices. A little girl in a dirty white dress came running out, and behind her in the half-lit doorway stood a small, elderly man. He wore a short-sleeved white shirt and a pair of beach shorts. This was the leaf doctor.

I hadn't known what to expect. I knew he wasn't going to be a full-blown Voodoo *houngan* of any sort. The ritual and lore of Martinique is basically Voodoo, but not like that of Haiti. Georges had been very clear: there would be no frothing ecstasies, no animal sacrifice, no walking on gilded splinters. I was disappointed all the same. Auguste looked like any old fisherman-farmer. He was a thin, knotty man with big hands that made cuffing movements as he spoke. His face was wrinkled, with a white stubble. His teeth were few and seemed to have grown bigger, like trees in a clearing. He was a little drunk, and since Georges was even now presenting him with a bottle of Mammy rum, he was likely to become more so.

We were introduced to a man and woman, Auguste's

assistants, and went inside. The shack was bare. There were a
couple of broken chairs and some boxes to sit on, a table with three
candles on it, and a rough stone fireplace. A low shelf in the corner
was covered with a cloth of the same vivid red as that on
Beauregard's cage. Bunches of dried leaves and roots hung from the
rafters. On the wall there was a calendar advertising a French
shipping line. It was turned to the current month—wintry vistas of
the Auvergne—but was several years out of date.

The main impact of the room was not seen but smelt:
candlewax and dust, spices and herbs, aromatic smoulderings from
the fire, and other things impossible to guess at.

Auguste had greeted me with a cordial grunt. But I soon
gathered he objected to my presence. His Creole was even faster
than Jo's, but I caught the word *blanc* a couple of times, and *métro*,
which is what they call a Frenchman. Jo told him I was English, and
a writer, and anyway I would have to stay because I couldn't find my
way back alone. Georges produced more offerings from his bag: a
pack of untipped Gauloises, a pair of custard-apples from his own
orchard and a wad of old-fashioned ten-franc bills.

Auguste swiftly lost interest in the troublesome *blanc*. He
began to count the money, now and then licking his thumb with a
large pink tongue. The money was not enough. There was an
argument, Auguste itemizing expenses on his thick fingers,
Georges shrugging and muttering, *'Eh, beh, Bon Dieu!'* It all
seemed something of a formality, and soon enough Georges pulled
out a few more francs from his back pocket.

Everything was in order. Auguste said, *'Bai-moin ti-poule.'* Jo
took the cloth off the cage, undid the wicker latch, and reached the
rooster out into the leaf doctor's drowsy shack.

Auguste held Beauregard gently in both hands. He looked
him over, viewed him at angles, as if he were thinking of
making a purchase.

'He has a good small head,' he observed.

'Yes, he has the gypsy face,' Jo replied.

'His eye is fierce.'

'Yes, eye of fire.'

The rhapsody continued. His thigh was fat, his legs were hard, his claws sharp. His cock-a-doodle-doo was *comme il faut* (a cock that crows too loud or too often is thought to be showy, not a true fighter).

I had heard the legends of his prowess, both pugnacious and amatory, but I had never been much impressed by Beauregard's appearance. He was a small, scraggy specimen compared to the barnyarders of England. His head was peppered with scars and puncture marks, souvenirs of the pit. The newest scabs were speckled white with alum used to cauterize the wounds. His docked wattles and misshapen feathers gave him a shifty, down-at-heel air. He looked like the avian equivalent of someone who would gladly cheat you of your last *sou*. But to the expert eye he was clearly a thing of grace, the stuff of cockpit legend.

Auguste turned him round and peered at his rump. Where the lower tail feathers had been clipped, the flesh showed through a livid red. Auguste seemed pleased.

'*Eh beh, eh beh, fout' i bel cul rouge!*' he said. What a lovely red arse he's got.

'*Rouge courage, rose peur,*' agreed Jo.

Auguste walked to the centre of the hut. He held the rooster with outstretched arms. He pointed him to each of the four corners of the hut. Then he turned him round and stared into his red eye and began to mumble something in a fast, high voice. Most of this was unintelligible to me. I heard the names of Beauregard and Tonton, and the word *gaguerre*, Creole term for cockfight. I heard snatches of dog Latin and a formulary phrase repeated many times: *Ouvri barrié pour li-passé*. Open the gates and let him pass . . .

I whispered to Georges, 'What's he saying?'

'He is praying to Gaspard.'

'Who is Gaspard?' An angry look from Jo. I had promised 'no fool questions'.

Georges smiled. Gaspard was a spirit, he whispered, a *capitaine des zombis* who had special influence in cock fights.

Auguste now went to the table. He asked for matches and lit the three candles on the table. There was old wax beneath them. He mumbled another imprecation in his high, irritable voice. The candles, I later learned from Georges, were lit in honour of another captain of the zombies, Agrippa.

Charles Nicholl

Next came the preparing and applying of the magic *quimbois*. The red cloth was removed from the shelf in the corner, revealing many small piles: leaves, seeds, roots, pastes, parings and unguents. I recognized ginger and pimiento, and pods of vanilla, and the cuttings of purple verbena whose vivid blackcurrant aroma I had already smelt in the hut, but the rest were unknown to me. In the lore of *quimboiserie* I was illiterate. To one side lay a clutter of aged kitchenware—tin dishes, plastic funnels, bottles, dibbers. There was an ox tongue, looking none too fresh, in one of the dishes. Another contained chicken giblets.

Auguste began to mix and grind the ingredients in a small plastic bowl. He instructed his assistants, speaking in a calm, precise voice, like a surgeon. Dicings of tongue, a chicken's heart, a couple of pinches of scarlet snuff. Out of a small stoppered phial came a fine grey-black powder. I thought I caught a whiff of cordite. A dash of indigo, some cinnamon bark, a pale yellow liquid that may have been more of the little girl's pee. He spat into the mix from time to time and dropped ash from his cigarette. The end product was a liverish blue-brown sludge. Some white spirit was added to make it easier to apply.

Beauregard was brought once more from his cage. Auguste scooped *quimbois* from the bowl and smeared it over him, working it in between his feathers. Beauregard protested. The *quimbois* stung his newly plucked skin, and though Jo held him tightly he twice managed to peck Auguste's hand. The leaf doctor just laughed, showing yellow teeth like tombstones.

We left around midnight. Jo and Georges argued. It seemed there was another ceremony which Jo had wanted Auguste to do. Georges hadn't wanted it. It was a bad ceremony, he said, and anyway Auguste charged too much. It involved the use of *poussière de mort*, 'dead man's dust', taken from a grave in the local cemetery.

The night had grown heavy and hot. Suddenly Jo stopped. '*Couté, couté*,' he said. He cupped his hand to his ear and rolled his eyes. Above the night sounds I heard a strange, low, creaking kind of moan. It might have been the wind, but none was blowing. It might have been a woman groaning softly by the roadside.

Jo saw my startled face and doubled up in laughter. Georges said, 'It's OK, it's just the banana trees.' At certain times of the year

236

they groan as the sap is forced down into the fruit. It was the groaning of the *bananiers*, nothing more.

Sunday afternoon and the cockpit was filling up fast. A fat mama in polka dots took the money at the door: ten francs for the front row, eight for the rest. She moved with surprising agility to collar two boys trying to worm up through the benches without paying.

The cockpit, Le Pitt Atlantique, was a circular wooden structure covered with a tin roof. From the outside it resembled one of those early playhouses you see in maps of Elizabethan London. There were no walls, just tiered wooden benches around the arena, which was a circle of packed earth about thirty feet in diameter. The pit stood on land owned by Georges's father. We had eaten lunch at his home: rum punch on the balcony, fresh snapper and plantain cakes. In the front room were reproduction Gauguins and a row of encyclopaedias locked in a glass-fronted bookcase. He had lost the key some years ago. 'I'm too old to learn anyway,' he said.

We went inside the cockpit. There was shade and the hum of voices. Smoke drifted in from the fry-stalls outside. Around the arena the faces were packed in tight. So many black faces under so many hats: trilbies and Panamas and *bakoua* straw hats; Jo's old topi and Georges's orange baseball cap with 'Honda' written on it; the women's headscarves of bright Madras cotton, knotted to signal a heart that is free (one knot), a heart that is taken (two knots), a heart that is anybody's (three knots). Some of the women were so lovely you hardly dared to count.

The luminaries of Vauclin life were there: Pierre the melancholy butcher; Ti-Noël the boat-builder, another of Jo's candidates for the richest man in the village; Monsieur Fragonard the policeman, a small pallid Parisian said to be on the run from his past; and Christophe, the *patron* of the hotel, big and jovial and bearded like a pirate, cradling in his arms his pet mongoose, Papetu, whose trick was to bite my toes beneath the dining table until I delivered bits of bread and cheese.

The bookmakers were ranged along the front row, dapper in pressed shirts and sunglasses, with thin cigars between their teeth. Bets were shouted from all sides, computed in the old French style, *cent* for one franc and *mille* for ten. Hands waved fans of banknotes, hands did tic-tac, hands wiped the sweat from gamblers' brows.

The first bout was about to get underway. Two cocks were brought into the arena. They were 500-gram bantam cocks: the smallest birds go first. Their weights were confirmed, and chalked up on a blackboard. A wooden box, fastened to the roof by a rope and pulley, was let down into the arena. It contained a candle, a cake of wax, some cotton wool, a bottle of alcohol and sticking plaster. First each cock was swabbed with alcohol to clean any grease or remnants of *quimbois* from its feathers. Next some wax was heated with the candle and pressed onto the cock's heel. Spurs were fastened on with the wax and held in place by the plaster.

The spurs were steel, about two inches long, tapering to a vicious point. Jo had told me that in the old days they used to be silver, but now 'no one has the knowledge to make them.' The spur was fixed to the shaved-down stub of the cock's natural spur. The handler must be careful to get the angle exactly right. The action of a cock when 'heeling' an opponent brings the spurs close to his own head, and there is the risk of him gashing himself if they're wrongly mounted.

The preliminaries were complete. The referee was satisfied. *'Hors la gageure!'* The handlers carried the cocks out of the ring. The box of accoutrements was winched back to the roof. Two little doors opened at opposite sides of the arena. The cocks were ushered through, the doors slammed shut behind them, and the fight was underway.

It is gone five when Beauregard and Tonton at last take the ring. The light softens outside the Pitt Atlantique, but inside the heat is raging. A succession of cocks—Montagne, Danse, Emmanuel, Passepartout, Ti-Diable ('Little Devil'), Longé Diole ('Stick out your beak') and many others—have come and gone, and fought their brief encounters, one lasting no more than forty seconds before he was pierced through the lung and tossed to the mounting pile of corpses in the corner.

But no thought of these now as—weighed, swabbed, spurred and given a quick shot of *rhum vieux* through a straw—the two old campaigners enter the cockpit.

Tonton is brown with orange streaking on his saddle-feathers.

His true name is Napoleon, fitting enough since Trois Ilets is the birthplace of Marie-Joseph Taschers, better known as Napoleon's Josephine. Tonton—'Uncle'—is a nickname often given to veteran fighters. His handler is a big man. He has a flat, squarish face, the look of a hammerhead shark.

The opening of the fight follows an established pattern. First, the sizing-up. Beauregard is nonchalant. He saunters round his patch of the pit as if it were a corner of his own well-appointed pen. He pecks at a few imaginary morsels in the dust. He peers with mild curiosity at the antics of the crowd. He doesn't seem to have noticed Tonton at all. Tonton's style is different. He is brisk, muscular, confident. He patrols his patch, limbers, flexes his wings. I half expect him to do a few quick press-ups.

By degrees the combatants draw closer to each other. Tonton moves in a busy zigzagging path. He's got energy to spare. Beauregard is still casual, musing, his little tonsured head moving back and forth like a well-oiled mechanism. As they meet the noise mounts. A contingent of visitors from Trois Ilets is packed in close to the entrance, battling to be heard above the home crowd. *'Va, va, salope!'* shout the Vaucliniers. *'Bai-li, bai-li, bai-li!'* bellow the Insulaires.

The opening flurries are exploratory. They are warning shots: a quick angry mingling, a dance of feathers. The crowd affects to find this hilarious. There are shouts of *'Yo baissé comme ti-fi!'* (They're kissing like little girls) and *'Yo chanté pomme, Bon Dieu!'* (They're sweet-talking each other).

The cocks separate. In more natural circumstances this first scuffle might have settled the argument. But there is no room for diplomacy in the *gageure*. Beauregard seems to turn away, as if to return to his corner. Then suddenly he is springing, up and at Tonton. Tonton rises too, but a second late. There's a vicious session of hacking and pecking. For a moment they hang there, a blur of wings and dust high above the ground. They push away and fall. Beauregard lands with absurd aplomb, while Tonton lurches down in a lopsided movement. First blood: Beauregard.

Down in the handlers' area Jo is haggard-faced. He shouts, waves his topi, runs a hand through his cropped grey hair. Georges is silent, leaning his elbows on the wooden rim of the arena, chewing fast on some gum. Across the other side Hammerhead from Trois

Ilets looks worried. He waves a huge fist at the cocks, issues dark ultimata.

Beauregard has the best of the second skirmish but Tonton takes the third. He produces an extraordinary swivelling movement in mid-air and delivers a deadly reverse-heel kick. His spurs rake down Beauregard's neck. Of the cock's two weapons, beak and spurs, it is the spurs which are the killers. The beak can blind, and it can finish off a downed cock, but its main use in the *gageure* is to get hold of the opponent's head so that the spurs can do their business. Beauregard reels away. There is blood and torn skin on his back. For a moment it seems that Tonton might turn the tables.

It is not to be. Tonton is tough and cunning, but after half a dozen skirmishes there is little doubt. Both birds are dazed now, but it is Beauregard who is relentless, wheeling into the next attack while Tonton is still recovering from the last.

This is the finale. Tonton is exhausted. His movements are weary. He has forgotten why he is here. A few last jabs with the spur and he is down. Beauregard turns on his heel, struts to the crowd, punch-drunk. His beak is full of blood and feathers, and the feathers flutter out as he crows a few cracked war-cries. The red light flashes on and off ten times and Tonton is counted out.

The fight has lasted four minutes. People call, *'Net, net, net!'* — the equivalent of the football crowd's chant of 'Ea-sy!'—as the handlers run on to gather up the roosters. Tonton is still moving: perhaps he'll pull through. The bookies are beginning to pay out. Jo examines Beauregard, looking for the bad wounds. He puts the cock's head in his mouth and sucks it to clean off the blood, and for a moment there's a silence, a silence with the tight feel of ritual, and when the noise comes flooding back I find myself shaken and sweating.

I did not think I was that kind of person: another voice yelling for blood, another face craning to see the kill.

I walk down to the handlers' area. They're mobbing Jo, thrusting drinks at him, brandishing their winnings. Everyone looks happy. Beauregard is back in his cage, quivering and manic. The blood on his torn back is the colour of the cloth on his cage, the colour of the cloth on the leaf doctor's shelf.

PEREGRINE HODSON
CRASH

I n July 1987 my Aunt Ennie died. I remembered her only as an occasional visitor from London during my childhood, who always wore the same grey-and-white speckled tweed overcoat. She was eighty-three.

I was a beneficiary of her will. She left me a small portfolio of shares, invested in blue-chip companies: General Universal Stores, Shell Transport, ICI and Cadbury Schweppes. Not a young man's portfolio: no Japanese warrants or call options on the Dow-Jones, no companies in the unlisted securities market or futures contracts against gold. The shares had been chosen by my great aunt's advisers at her bank and were correspondingly impersonal: safe, mediocre, boring. Until probate was granted the shares were in limbo and I could do nothing with them. I wasn't concerned; the market was buoyant and forecasts were optimistic.

F RIDAY 9 OCTOBER: It is still dark outside. I lean out of bed to switch on the light. Nothing happens. Damn. I stumble towards the bathroom and flick the light switch. No electricity. Damn.

The streets are littered with debris. I come to a house with a gaping hole in the roof, as if a massive fist has slammed into it, leaving the walls intact, and I begin to grasp the dimensions of the storm. Everywhere the roads are covered with fallen branches, and scattered with fragments of tiles, the remains of twisted umbrellas and crumpled sheets of plastic.

At the bank I sweep the electronic pass-key across the door and it opens with a satisfying click. The dealing room seems empty, and I switch on the screens at my desk. I tap through the electronic pages to read the market reports. Unusually, some of the shares still have no prices, even though it is past nine o'clock and the market has already opened.

I see Matthew light a cigarette. The stub from the previous one is still smouldering. Matthew sits at the desk next to mine and sometimes, when there is a lull in the market, like now, we talk. Since the beginning of the year he has made seven or eight million pounds for the firm, maybe more, which is why he earns as much as a Cabinet minister or a general. I admire his single-mindedness and determination, and he sees me, perhaps, as a latecomer to banking and occasionally calls me 'young Perry' although I am almost ten years older than him. He says this with mocking affection and it amuses us both. Sometimes he asks what I was doing at his age, but I avoid telling him about Benares or the stars over the Castle of Assassins because I imagine it will remind him of the price he has paid in the past for what he is earning now. He compares what I have with what he has, and wonders who has made the better deal. Neither of us knows the answer.

I switch on the screen and check the prices of Aunt Ennie's shares. The choice of solid, multinational companies implies a philosophy of life, and the size of the holdings reflects the experience of another, older generation: Edwardian prosperity, the Great War, the 1920s, the Crash and the Depression. The portfolio is almost all that remains of a life which spanned the century, a record of economic and historical cycles. The thought of selling the shares seems disrespectful, like burning the letters of the dead. However, the market has been softening over the last two months and people are beginning to say that the bull market is over. Matthew, naturally, thinks I should sell immediately and buy some options.

I look around. There is an air of unreality in the dealing room. It is how I imagine the pace of activity in a bank before there was screen trading: unhurried figures walking between desks and leisurely telephone conversations between men who went to school together. Back then a gentleman could earn a reasonable income if he read the business pages of *The Times*. Now it's different. But now it is the age of computerized banking and the systems have gone down.

SATURDAY 10 OCTOBER: I get up late and read the *Financial Times* over breakfast. The major headline is the weather. The Lex column notes: 'In the way that unnatural events accompany murders in Shakespeare, the stormy weather which kept trading in the London stock market to a minimum yesterday might have been paralleled to the turbulence in the world securities markets.' I check the prices of Aunt Ennie's shares.

General Universal Stores	£14 $^3/_{16}$
Shell Transport	£13 $^1/_{16}$
ICI	£15 $^7/_{16}$
Cadbury Schweppes	277p

They are beginning to fall.

MONDAY 19 OCTOBER: The dealing room is crowded. Voices are pitched high, and Matthew is eating a bacon sandwich. He mumbles something but I cannot hear what he is saying. I switch on the middle screen at my desk: Screen 2 SEAQ. This is the screen which displays the current prices of the *Financial Times* Stock Exchange 100—the index of the largest UK companies. Company names are reduced to three letters with the current share price given alongside. If the share is above the previous day's closing price, both company and price will be displayed in blue letters, and if below, in red. When there is no change, the letters and numbers are green. When the price is rising, numbers flash blue, and when it is falling, red. Today the electronic page is almost entirely red. Here and there red figures are pulsing, marking further decline.

'Exciting stuff,' says Matthew. He leans forward and wipes grease from his mouth with a paper napkin. 'Looks like we're in for a bit of a drama. The FTSE 100 is already off a hundred points.'

The flashing red numbers re-arrange themselves, like soot particles glowing and sparkling at the back of a chimney. The screen glows and flickers.

'Wall Street took a knock on Friday,' says Matthew, 'and everybody's shitting themselves. Bye-bye bull market.' He shows more excitement than alarm. I feel the same. We are watching a stock market crash: it has the same compelling horror as the jerky film of the explosion of the *Hindenburg* airship in the 1930s. For a while the numbers stop pulsing. Here and there a share flashes blue as a few buyers come back into the market. But then the figures start flashing red again and join up with one another in irregular clusters until the screen is once again a mass of glowing red.

It is difficult to make sense of what is happening. Selling comes in waves, the onset of fever. I remember Aunt Ennie's shares and call the Probate Office. Someone goes to find out what is happening. There is a long wait, and then I'm told the Office is unable to say when probate will be granted. It's suggested I telephone again in a few days.

Christine sits on the opposite side of the desk. She is in her late thirties and her face is permanently drawn. She doesn't look a happy woman. 'I saw this months ago,' she says, 'it was *tout clair*. I have had all my monies in the bank since the summer. No one could support the pressure of the bull market. Everyone's been wanting it to end: it's a collective death-wish, like being in love with Thanatos.'

Christine took a course of Jungian therapy after she divorced her husband.

'How about you,' she continues, 'are you out?'

I tell her about the shares in my great aunt's estate, explain how they are locked in the market. It's like being trapped in a falling lift, I say. 'That's tough,' she exclaims, with no change of expression.

I remember that the authoritative banker is expected to be wealthy or fortunate or intelligent, and preferably all three. I ought to say something clever but my mind is a blank. I smile, Japanese-style, and head for the coffee machine.

It's easy to see who is heavily invested in the market and who is on the sideline. I see two or three people with glass grins. Those on the sideline, by contrast, are enjoying their role. Everyone says something different: 'Cash is king'; 'Wait for the bounce'; 'Convertibles are sensible, except you don't know about interest rates'; 'Wait to see what happens in New York—the program trading may push it the other way.'

But nobody knows what is happening. It's like a holiday, like the Feast of Misrule. Everyone is equal. The old hand who has been watching the market for twenty-five years and the school-leaver who only shaves three times a week are as wise as each other. Neither of them has experienced a crash of these proportions. Everyone is a lamb in the slaughterhouse.

Phillip is in his mid-thirties. He's five-foot-three and unmarried. Not rich, not lucky, so he has to be intelligent. But he has a problem. He wasn't intelligent enough to get out of the markets, so now he's telling everyone: 'I'm not selling. You're all crazy. It's an aberration. You can do what you like.' He has a day-glo golf ball which he throws in the air and catches, throws in the air and catches, throws in the air so that it almost touches the ceiling: hope, despair, hope, despair, hope—and he fumbles the catch.

Brian is one of the big boys. He's in his early forties and he's been riding the bull market for the last decade. He's a financial trouble-shooter. His face is a reddish pink and his eyes protrude, as if he has a thyroid imbalance. Brian is rich. Everyone knows he has a lot of money: Brian tells them. He shows people photographs of his estate in Wales, casually lets slip details of his holdings in certain shares, and buys muddy abstracts by successful artists. Socially, he is very brittle. He is uncertain which class he belongs to, a problem common among bankers. Earning more doesn't make the problem go away unless you're saving for 'fuck you' money. A month ago Brian told me about 'fuck you' money. 'It's the amount of money you need to be able to say "Fuck you" to anyone.' Brian reckoned the current amount to be three million pounds.

Brian is wearing a doll-like expression: his eyebrows arch and his mouth bends in a simpering smile. I've seen him smile in the same way while listening to a girl describe how she fell from a horse and broke her collar-bone. He is curiously silent and at eleven-thirty announces he is going out for a long lunch. It doesn't sound heroic.

Max, another dealer, looks off-colour. He's tapping through the pages of SEAQ and no one makes jokes in his vicinity, as if there was an invisible cloud around him. 'He had a few long positions,' someone tells me by the coffee machine, and the words have an icy ring. I press the number for creamy whipped coffee with sugar: 62. A little sign lights up, saying, 'Your coffee is being prepared.'

TUESDAY 20 OCTOBER: The alarm wakes me earlier than usual. I look at the *Financial Times*: ROUT ON WALL STREET LEADS TO RECORD FALLS. The headline is already history. I see also that Aunt Ennie's shares are plunging.

General Universal Stores	£11 $^3/_8$
Shell Transport	£11 $^5/_8$
ICI	£14 $^1/_{16}$
Cadbury Schweppes	245p

Click. The screens are red—completely red. No one can get through on the screens. No trades. No one is talking. I try to take notes. I want to describe what it's like to be sitting at the centre of a stock market crash.

It's fairly quiet. It's like dropping a stone off a cliff and waiting. It's all happening in slow motion. Here at the screens there's no panic; there's time to talk to your neighbour. But what do you say? Matthew says, 'There's so many sharks out there waiting to leg you over. They laugh like buggery when they shaft you.'

No one knows where the bottom is. The FTSE 100 is already another fifty off, and still going down.

It's different from how I thought it might be. The market is in free fall, but here in the dealing room there are no wild-eyed figures screaming into telephones, no men in waistcoats with watch-chains sobbing that they are ruined, none of the clichés of stock market catastrophe.

The number flash and blink relentlessly. Minute by minute, tens of millions of pounds are vanishing. Silently. The market has become an alien entity with its own destiny and momentum. We are watching a titanic process which none of us understand; the numbers seem to have a life of their own. I am thinking of a line from a song by Bob Dylan: '*This is what infinity must be like after a while.*' Matthew is silent. I must snap out of it.

I see Tom empty his ashtray into a bin. He likes to keep his ashtray clean. He's been trading equities for twenty years, makes jokes about the young men in their shirts like deck-chairs, and he's seen it all before. Almost. He says, 'What can I do for you, sir?' Tom calls me 'sir', although he's twice my age. He's one of the old school: joined the firm as a messenger after the war. Now he's one of the top traders on the London market. He leans forward and speaks into his desk intercom. 'John,' he says. 'Check if we've cleared our positions on Glaxo. The stock's heading south in a big way.'

I think of Aunt Ennie as Tom turns to me again. He says he's getting too old for this kind of caper. He's thinking of retirement. 'Excuse me a moment,' he says, pressing down the button on the intercom. 'John, what the hell's happening with *those fucking Glaxo?*'

Tom tells me he wishes he could take up painting again. Or spend more time with his fish. He collects coi carp.

WEDNESDAY 21 OCTOBER: The situation has lost its novelty. My eyes ache from staring into the red screens. Someone in the office is calling up a graph of the performance of the London market. The display takes some thirty seconds, and then the graph is complete. There are the ominous twin peaks of the 'double-top', the classic harbinger of disaster, and there, like the first shock of a massive earthquake recorded on a seismograph, is the jagged downstroke: the crash.

The prices of Aunt Ennie's shares are still falling and I try once again to ring the Probate Office. There is no reply.

NOTES FROM ABROAD

Cricket in Samoa
Gavin Young

'*K*irikiti, kirikiti* . . . Come, come! . . . Quicklee!'
'Well, into the car then.'
But young Fili, digger of taro, hewer of coconuts, wasn't in that much of a hurry to watch his father Tolu playing cricket. We had only driven a short way before he began to pummel my shoulder in a well-meaning way and begged me to stop.

'Yes, Fili?'

He gave me what he evidently considered his most winning smile. He had remembered something, he said. His friend Etawati was being tattooed by a famous artist a little way off the road. Could we pick him up?

I bumped the little Subaru off the dust track through a fringe of coconut palms and across a short stretch of uneven red earth praying we wouldn't sink up to the axles. The tattoo-artist's lozenge-shaped house stood there, its cock-eyed roof thatched raggedly with sugar leaves and supported by spindly pillars of giant fern. Etawati sprang grinning from the house and into the car. Like the Samoans with me, he wore nothing but a lavalava, the brightly coloured 'kilt' of the islands. He spoke rapidly to Fili. He hadn't, I noticed, a mark on him.

'Well?' I asked Fili. 'Where's the tattoo?'

'Etawati says he has no money for tattoo,' Fili whispered, adding in wheedling tones, 'maybe you can give . . .?'

'Maybe,' I said, sensing a plot. 'But if at all, later. After the cricket'—and I saw them exchange victorious winks.

'Now *kirikiti*,' Tolu growled impatiently.

'*Kirikiti*,' Fili agreed, adding in my ear, 'quickly!'—as though picking up Etawati had been a tiresome idea of mine all along.

I had seen Samoans playing *at* cricket—you see small boys swinging makeshift bats in front of three upright twigs in almost every village clearing—but never a real game at close quarters. I knew there were taboos connected with it because once, pausing to watch a game in the walled grounds of one of the island's religious colleges, I had been about to perch on the wall when a young theological student with a stern, God-fearing expression strode up. It was forbidden, he said, to touch the wall. And under that Dr Arnold of Rugby gaze I had slunk back to the car and driven off.

Tolu had talked of the Samoan passion for *kirikiti*; a fever they had caught from the New Zealanders who ruled Western Samoa under League of Nations mandate for fifty years after 1914. He'd even displayed his wounds. I had been adopted by his family (he had a wife, four girls and two boys) soon after wandering into his remote part of the island, and he had insisted I stay with them. He had come home soon after with a bloody white cloth wrapped round his calf, and through his twenty-year-old son Fili, who spoke fair school English, he had explained that, running to take a catch in a cricket match, he had tripped over a lump of coral. Coral cuts turn septic with extraordinary speed but the pride of a Samoan chief was strong in Tolu and he went about his work planting taro and cutting sugar as if nothing had happened.

I turned the little car on to a narrower track, so closely hedged by undergrowth that foliage slapped its sides, and now and again I had to stop to allow people to squeeze by on horses laden with coconuts. Soon the track dipped and became stony and for five minutes we bumped steeply down towards the sea. There the ground levelled out to a beach of white sand. Fifty-foot palms with slender silver trunks shook tousled green heads and blue banks of morning glories skirted the greener blue waters of a lagoon where the sea lapped lazily over a reef. Under Tolu's orders, I stopped the car near a white steepled church. I heard the unmistakable clunk of ball on bat and from a house the sound of a radio choir singing a popular South Sea spiritual that I knew must come from Pago-Pago in nearby American Samoa:

I want to be ready
I want to be ready
I want to be ready
To walk to Jerusalem
Just . . . like . . . John

Bare-chested men were running about a clearing with two wickets on it and, above the cries of the cricketers, a fruity American voice intoned, 'The Revival Time Choir comes to you now with a song entitled "Eternal Life". Sing along as Brother Maclellan leads us.' *Whack!*—for the moment it seemed wiser to duck than to sing along with Brother Maclellan. With incredible velocity, a cricket ball hissed past us like a large bullet and vanished into the undergrowth. Two muscular fielders thundered by in pursuit clutching the hems of their lavalavas above their knees and began rooting about in the bush while the two batsmen sprinted back and forth between makeshift stumps at each end of the strip of coconut matting that represented the pitch. A storm of cheering rose from the branches of surrounding trees where spectators perched, bright patches of colour half-hidden by the leaves, like bizarre inmates of some tropical aviary.

It took five minutes to retrieve the ball, which promptly disappeared again. *Whack!*—it vanished over a thatched roof. *Whack!*—this time into the morning glories. *Whack!*—now like an unexploded missile among a family of pigs near the church. No blocking here, I could see, no stonewalling, no fancy footwork, no prissy prodding, glancing or gliding. Every unpadded batsman was a mahogany Botham in full-blooded spate, every stroke a mighty, head-severing sweep of a battle-axe.

Samoans are large people: tall, solid, built to kill or tote sacks of coconuts by the hundredweight. At Tolu's age —say, forty—they tend to corpulence, but the hard plantation work keeps them strong and agile. As viewed from the pavilion at Lord's cricket ground in London, the Mecca of this curious game, the Samoan nature is probably not one that lends itself to the game's finer elements. Nor do the local rules encourage aesthetic play: in fact, it's a bit of a scrimmage. On this particular day, for example, I saw twenty or thirty players, and Fili added an extra puzzle by remarking, 'Those men under the coconuts—more players. May play later.' Reserves, I supposed he meant. It seemed that in theory a game could go on for hours or even days with fifty or sixty batsmen queueing up for a bash. But I knew this wasn't so. Alan Grey, the manager of his mother Aggie's famous hotel in Apia and a former trainer of the Samoan rugby side, had reassured me: 'You see, with no pads players don't fiddle around much in defensive play. They swing the bat mightily, hitting sixes and fours, but they often miss too and naturally wickets tumble pretty fast. I've seen sides out for a mere twenty-three runs or so.'

There is no leg-before-wicket rule in the Samoan game and little need for one, for who would be fool enough to risk his bare legs and unprotected groin? You either hit the ball and make runs or are caught, or miss it and are bowled. I saw several batsmen, including poor Tolu, struck on the back or upper thigh by fast rising balls, and in true warrior tradition they simply rubbed the spot and stoically awaited the next ball.

The game went on. Balls flew toward the beach or into dense jungle. Enthusiastic young fielders tumbled head over heels in the morning glories. Village elders, large, heavy-breasted, critical men, lay in the shade on cushions discussing the course of play like contented sea lions on their favourite rocks.

The reserves waited expectantly with their bats before them on the grass and I went over and picked up one or two of these great chunks of wood—huge things that strained my wrists when I swung them at imaginary balls. Long, three feet or more, with the slim shape of baseball bats, they had three narrow striking faces with sharp edges instead of the conventional cricket bat's single, rectangular face, and their handles were tightly bound with strands of coconut fronds. Because of their weight and length, it took the forearms and wrists of a Samoan warrior to handle them.

These bats resembled warriors' clubs—had in fact developed from Samoan war-clubs, but not far. The young batsmen posed for my camera shouldering their bats and assuming fierce, warlike expressions. Not so long ago they would have been fighting, not playing cricket. They would have flung their enemies' heads, not cricket balls, before those reclining elders and with each one have shouted, 'I have taken a man!' with all the pride of a young Englishman celebrating his first Test century.

Such things continued into the early years of this century. Head-hunting, not cricket, was the national Samoan sport in Robert Louis Stevenson's time, and from the woods surrounding Vailima, his house at the foot of Mount Vaea, the sound of drums and war-cries interrupted his efforts to chronicle David Balfour's adventures in the misty north of Britain. Once, friendly warriors called him out to admire a set of newly cut heads and—horror!—one of them proved to be that of a village maiden. Much abashed by this taboo decapitation, the young heroes wrapped the head in a costly silk handkerchief and returned it to the girl's grieving family with profuse apologies. Such things the Stevenson family—even old Mrs Stevenson—took in its stride. Louis actually approved of the ferocious 'hedge-wars' that swirled around Vailima, believing that the race he described as 'God's sweetest work' was purged and regenerated through battle.

Several decades of earnest Christian missionary endeavour have failed to eliminate the Samoans' warrior temperament. In one quite recent match, Alan Grey told me, a villager was bowled and refused to leave the crease. 'In a fury, he smashed his wicket with his bat and refused to apologise—a terrible insult to the host village. A mob of enraged spectators took off after him, a kid felled him with a stone, another spectator got a knife or a machete, and they killed him. Later on everyone was terribly sorry. Too late, of course.'

Today at least one small part of God's sweetest work had said to hell with cricket. Fili lay with his back to the action lazily watching the waves on the reef. One or two village boys were splashing each other in the lagoon and further along the beach I saw Manino, Tolu's wife, with her daughter Emma, searching the shallows for shellfish and crabs.

The midday heat had been still, wet and oppressive, but as the afternoon wore on a welcome breeze stirred from the lagoon.

People began to emerge from the surrounding plantations and to converge on the little white open church. An organ played a bouncy tune; large ladies in ankle-length white dresses flowed in and out chatting and laughing loudly and patting each other's children. A dog slept in an aisle. Half-hidden by vases of white flowers, the pastor intoned in soft Samoan sing-song, '*Ona faapea atu ai lea o le motu o tagato, O Jesu lenei le perofeta mai Nasareta i Kalilain.*' A card in my pew gave the reference Mataio XXI, and when I looked up St Matthew's Gospel later I found, 'When he entered Jerusalem, the whole city was agitated. "Who is this?" they asked. The crowd replied, "This is the Prophet Jesus from Nazareth in Galilee."' It didn't seem to have much to do with our afternoon of cricket.

The game was drawing to a close. Soon Tolu ran up puffing and sweating. 'No injuries, Tolu?' He laughed. He had hit two boundaries; six runs each time. Watched by a small, interested crowd, Manino and Emma loaded their sackful of crabs, cockles and cowries into the car. Etawati, Fili's friend from the tattooist's, rode up on horseback, wearing a T-shirt stencilled with 'Hellaby's Pacific Corned Beef', and presented me with two Pacific pigeons— handsome birds with green backs and long tails.

At the top of the escarpment the sun was lost behind the mountain and the great trees were full of shadows. Lights appeared on hillsides veiled by the blue-grey smoke of evening fires. Like a last fragment of sunlight, a brilliant yellow bird flitted across the track, and a fruit bat flapped heavily overhead. Behind me Tolu belched richly, anticipating the meal Manino would give us: the cockles, the spotted crabs, slices of taro with coconut cream, a piglet baked in banana and breadfruit leaves. He would sit on his haunches, happy with the thought of those two sixes, crunching in his teeth the charred heads of Etawati's Pacific pigeons as slowly and sensuously as if they were the last pigeons in paradise.

Notes on Contributors

Václav Havel's latest play *Temptation* is published by Faber & Faber in March. **Jonathan Raban** has recently completed a trip visiting the ports of western Europe, to be the subject of a book, and has begun a new novel, of which 'Cyclone' is the opening. His piece 'Sea-Room' appeared in *Granta* 10, 'Travel Writing'. **Bill Bryson** is thirty-six years old. He is an Iowan who now lives in North Yorkshire, and the author of *The Penguin Dictionary of Troublesome Words*. He is currently at work on a book about returning to America. **Anton Shammas** is an Israeli Arab who lives in Jerusalem. 'The Retreat from Galilee' will be included in *Arabesques* that Viking Penguin publish later this year. **Fawwaz Traboulsi** was born in Beirut. He has translated works by Gramsci and John Reed, and written *On an Incurable Hope,* a diary of the siege of Beirut in 1982. He now lives in France. **Martha Gellhorn**'s latest book is *The View From the Ground,* a collection of her peace-time reporting, to be published this spring by Atlantic Monthly Press. **Norman Lewis** lives in Essex. *The Missionaries,* a study of the exploitation of the tribal peoples of Latin-America and Indochina, will be published in April. **Seamus Deane**'s 'Haunted' appeared in *Granta* 18. He is a member of *Field Day*, a publishing co-operative in Ireland, currently compiling a two-volume collection of Irish writing in 'English' literature. He is working on a book to be published next year by Granta Books. **Jeanette Winterson**'s most recent novel is *The Passion*, published in London by Bloomsbury and in New York by Atlantic Monthly Press. She is the winner of the John Llewelyn Rhys Memorial Award. **Jonathan Miller**'s most recent stage productions are *The Mikado* in Los Angeles and a revival of *One Way Pendulum* by N.F. Simpson in London. **Ian Hamilton**'s most recent book *Fifty Poems* was published last autumn. 'J. D. Salinger *versus* Random House, Inc.' is from *J. D. Salinger: A Writing Life* to be published in September in Britain by Heinemann. **Nicholas Shakespeare** is the literary editor of the *Daily Telegraph*, and has recently completed his first novel, set in Peru. **T. Coraghessan Boyle**'s most recent novel was *World's End.* He lives in Los Angeles. **Peregrine Hodson** works in banking. His 'A Journey into Afghanistan' was published in *Granta* 20, and he is now writing a book about Japan. **Charles Nicholl**'s account of his travels in Thailand and Burma will be published this autumn. He is the author of *The Fruit Palace,* about life in the cocaine underworld of Colombia. **Gavin Young** has just completed a history of the airline Cathay-Pacific, and is now writing a travel book based on the places described in Joseph Conrad's Far East novels.